DEC 1 8 2015

DREAM
CRUISING
DESTINATIONS

Adlard Coles Nautical

An imprint of Bloomsbury Publishing Plc

50 Bedford Square	1385 Broadway
London	New York
WC1B 3DP	NY 10018
UK	USA

www.bloomsbury.com

ADLARD COLES, ADLARD COLES NAUTICAL and the Buoy logo are trademarks of Bloomsbury Publishing Plc

First published 2015

British Library Cataloguing-in-Publication Data
A catalogue record for this book is available from the British Library.
Library of Congress Cataloguing-in-Publication data has been applied for.

ISBN: PB: 978-1-4081-8781-4
ePDF: 978-1-4729-1966-3
ePub: 978-1-4729-1967-0

2 4 6 8 10 9 7 5 3 1

Typeset in Myriad
Colour reproduction by Ivy Reprographic
Printed and bound in China by C&C Offset Printing Co

Created and produced for Adlard Coles Nautical by Ivy Contract
SENIOR EDITOR: Judith Chamberlain-Webber
DESIGN: Lisa McCormick

Please note that the maps are intended as a guide to the route and area only and are not accurate enough for any other use.

Note: while all reasonable care has been taken in the publication of this book, the publisher takes no responsibility for the use of the methods or products described in the book.

Bloomsbury Publishing Plc makes every effort to ensure that the papers used in the manufacture of our books are natural, recyclable products made from wood grown in well-managed forests. Our manufacturing processes conform to the environmental regulations of the country of origin.

To find out more about our authors and books visit www.bloomsbury.com. Here you will find extracts, author interviews, details of forthcoming events and the option to sign up for our newsletters.

DREAM
CRUISING
DESTINATIONS

Vanessa Bird

24 Classic Cruises
Mapped and Explored

ADLARD COLES NAUTICAL
BLOOMSBURY
LONDON · NEW DELHI · NEW YORK · SYDNEY

Contents

Introduction

If you could cruise anywhere in the world, where would you choose? Would you head for the cooler climes of Northern Europe, or the tropical heat of the southern hemisphere? Would you opt for island hopping, or prefer to go coastal cruising? Or does the excitement of a long-distance sail across huge expanses of sea, out of sight of land, entice?

The choice of places to explore around the world is simply vast and it can be a daunting prospect to make the decision about where to go, particularly if you don't know what to expect, or how much experience is required. But this is where *Dream Cruising Destinations* comes in. Within these pages is a snapshot of some of the finest cruising grounds from all around the world.

From the rugged beauty of the Western Isles of Scotland and Norway's Lofoten Islands to the glitz and glamour of the Côte d'Azur and the crystal-clear waters and gleaming white sandy beaches of the Seychelles, there is a destination here to suit all tastes. For those passionate about wildlife, the San Juan Islands off the USA's northwest Pacific coast or the underwater paradise of the Great Barrier Reef off the northeast coast of Australia are hard to better; while if it is a cruise through history that you are after, then head to Turkey or the Ionian Sea.

If you would prefer not to coastal hop or sail offshore, then there are plenty of inland waterways to choose from too. The French Canals, the Atlantic Intracoastal Waterway and Canada's Lake Huron

are all included as inland destinations worthy of exploration.

And if you seek more challenging long-distance adventures, then why not consider an Atlantic trade wind crossing, from the Canary Islands to St Lucia, or a circumnavigation of some of the most remote islands in the world? The final destination in the book is the Cook Islands, a Pacific archipelago that is for those who really want a taste of adventure. Visited by just 150 yachts each year, they are a true challenge for highly experienced sailors.

Once you have decided where you want to go, knowing a bit about the destination and what to expect can make the planning easier. Under each cruise there is a detailed route, either circular or linear, that encompasses the highlights of the area. The length of each route is a guideline that can be followed in its entirety or amended to suit your own requirements.

There is then information on the destinations themselves – where you can berth or anchor, where you can provision and what sites – historical, cultural and environmental – to see, as well as advice on how much experience you need and the level of skill that each destination requires. Although many of the routes are straightforward and through trouble-free waters, others require a certain level of skill to cope with challenges such as tricky tidal currents, rock-strewn channels and congested anchorages.

And finally, there is the all-important question of when to go, with each cruise detailing the time of the sailing season and what weather conditions to expect while you are out there.

It would be impossible to include every dream destination within one volume, but the intention is to provide you with enough ideas and information to turn your dreams into a reality. And provided you have a well-found boat, decent equipment and reasonable experience, there is no reason not to. As H Jackson Brown wrote in his 1990 book *P.S., I Love You*: 'Twenty years from now you will be more disappointed by the things that you didn't do than by the ones you did do. So throw off the bowlines. Sail away from the safe harbour. Catch the trade winds in your sails. Explore. Dream. Discover.'

VOYAGE 1

Scotland

THE WESTERN ISLES

The Western Isles, also known as the Outer Hebrides or Long Isle, are a chain of islands that lie off the northwest coast of Scotland. Spanning a length of around 104nm, the islands are a place of contrasts. The western shores are generally fringed with turquoise waters and magnificent white sandy beaches that stretch unbroken for miles, while the eastern shores are heavily punctuated with bays and sea lochs, which provide much to explore for cruising yachtsmen.

It can be a challenging place to sail – tricky tides and rock-strewn channels make it unsuitable for the inexperienced. However, destinations are within easy reach, so if conditions deteriorate then shelter can often quickly be found. Having said that, the key to exploring these islands is good weather. Without it, the full force of the Atlantic can be felt, so keep a close eye on the forecasts and only set sail if visibility is good.

Ashore there is much to appeal to the visitor too. The islands have been inhabited since the Mesolithic era. Today 15 of the islands are populated and many bear evidence of early settlements, including Allt Chrisal at Bentangaval on the Isle of Barra. For wildlife enthusiasts, the area is particularly rich, with 7,500 freshwater lochs and many of the offlying islands providing a birdwatcher's paradise, not to mention the 53 Sites of Special Scientific Interest (SSSIs) and the diverse range of fauna that can be found on the machairs, the low-lying arable or grazing land of the east coasts.

below Azure waters and sparkling white-sand beaches fringe the island of Harris.

The route

This route through the Western Isles is around 120nm in length, and starts at Castlebay on Barra, the southernmost inhabited island in the archipelago, which is a 35nm sail from the island of Coll off the northwest coast of Mull. From Castlebay, the route meanders up the heavily indented east coasts of the Western Isles, taking in Eriskay, South and North Uist and Harris, before ending up at Stornoway on Lewis, the northernmost harbour in the island chain, and the largest in the Outer Hebrides.

The beauty of this cruise is that although sailing conditions can prove tricky at times, the route offers plenty of diversions in the form of numerous bays and sea lochs that are fascinating places to explore and can provide good shelter, if required.

If you wish to extend the route further, trips to the remote Monach Isles, off North Uist's west coast, or the World Heritage Site of St Kilda, 42nm to the west of the Sound of Harris, can be undertaken. However, they should only be considered in the very best of conditions, as the exposed Atlantic coast of the Western Isles is not the place to be if the weather deteriorates, and it offers very few places of refuge.

If negotiating the 7nm-long Sound of Harris, the channel that separates North Uist and the Isle of Harris, and the main route to the west coasts of the island chain, be wary of fast-running tidal streams and unmarked rocks and reefs, and stick to the buoyed Stanton Channel.

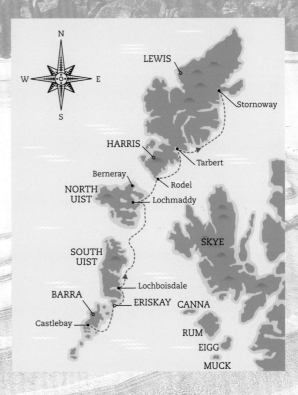

Destinations

Barra: The harbour of Castlebay at the start of this cruise is distinctive for Kisimul Castle, which sits atop the islet of Bagh a Chaisteil, immediately off the village. It's the only surviving medieval castle in the Western Isles, and was built by the MacNeil clan in 1427. Restored in the 1930s, it is now open to the public. Other sites of interest on Barra include Dualchas Heritage Centre and the archaeological monuments at Dùn Bharpa, Allt Chrisal and Dùn Cuier. The western side of the island also has some spectacular beaches.

Eriskay: Its name means 'Eric's Isle', and this small island is well known as the location of the foundering of the SS *Politician*. One thousand bottles of whisky are said to have been salvaged from the wreck by the locals on the island, which lies between Barra and South Uist. The harbour of Acarsaid Mhor, on the east side of the island, has two council-run visitors' moorings, and the beach at Coilleag a Phrionnsa is said to be where Bonnie Prince Charlie first set foot during the Jacobite Rising in 1745.

South Uist: The east coast of South Uist offers a fabulous cruising area for visitors, in the form of numerous bays and sea lochs. Stunning anchorages with reasonable shelter can be found in the lochs Skipport and Eynort, while visitors' moorings and facilities are available at Lochboisdale. The west coast is fringed with over 32km (20 miles) of white beaches, and the island is a haven for birdlife. The archaeological site at Cladh Hallan is the only UK site where prehistoric mummies have been found.

North Uist: At 303sq km (117 square miles), North Uist is slightly smaller than South Uist, but shares its sibling's beauty, with an east coast peppered with bays and sea lochs and a west coast fringed with beaches. Peat bogs and small lochs dominate the island, and the Taigh Chearsabhagh Museum & Arts Centre makes a great diversion. Visitors' moorings are available at Lochmaddy,

with further facilities due to open in 2014, and remote anchorages can be found at Loch Eport, 2½nm to the south, and off the low-lying Monach or Heisker Isles, which are located 4nm to the west.

Harris: The isles of Harris and Lewis are actually part of the same landmass, with Harris forming the southern part, separated from Lewis by a band of mountains. Famous for its tweed, Harris is also well known for its stunningly beautiful white-sand beaches and azure waters, fringed by the grassy plains of the machairs that are carpeted with colourful wild flowers in the summer. Visitors' moorings are available at Rodel on the east coast of the island, while anchorages can be found between here and Tarbert in an area known as the Bays.

Lewis: Beyond Harris lies Lewis and its rolling moors. Stornoway, on the northeast coast, is the largest harbour in the Western Isles, and has recently seen major development in the form of a 70-berth marina in the sheltered inner harbour. Facilities in Stornoway are very good. Remote yet sheltered anchorages can be found within the sea lochs to the south of the town.

Level of skill

The Western Isles have a fearsome reputation that deters many people from exploring them. Principally, this is as a result of the islands' exposed position on the edge of the Atlantic, and the consequent bad weather that can dominate this sea area. Certainly, the west coasts of the islands can be treacherous in strong winds, affording little shelter and few places of refuge, and crossing the Sea of Hebrides or North Minch from mainland Scotland can be a daunting prospect if the weather deteriorates. However, given the right conditions, it is an area rich with rewards. Although not one for the inexperienced sailor, anyone with moderate experience will find cruising in this area straightforward in settled conditions.

Close inshore the Sea of Hebrides is sheltered from much of the weather by the Western Isles, although on the mainland side of the sea it can feel more exposed, particularly as the relatively low-lying islands often remain hidden until halfway through the passage. Tidal streams in the Little Minch, the area between North Uist and the Isle of Skye, can be very challenging too, often running at up to 2½ knots on the eastern side of the channel, so crossing from Canna to Barra, where the tidal streams flow more slowly, is often preferable, despite the greater distance.

Around the islands, tidal streams can at times be unpredictable, and a close examination of the chart and good pilotage skills are essential in order to familiarize yourself with the area and any rocks or reefs. This is particularly important in the sounds of Barra and Harris, the main routes through to the Atlantic, parts of which are shallow and littered with unmarked rocks. Be aware too, of the comings and goings of fishing boats and inter-island ferries.

As moorings for visitors are minimal within the islands, it is also important that anyone visiting has a good knowledge of anchoring. Many of the sea lochs that pepper the islands' east coasts offer good shelter but demand confident anchoring skills.

When to go

May to September offers the best time of year to explore the Western Isles. May and June tend to be drier, and July and August warmer. The islands' northerly latitude means that it is still not as warm as destinations farther to the south, although the hours of daylight will be significantly longer. Having said that, the climate in the Western Isles is generally milder than much of the UK, primarily as a result of the North Atlantic Drift, the northernmost part of the Gulf Stream, which helps to maintain temperatures several degrees higher than those on the east coast of Scotland.

While visitor numbers do increase during high summer, the Western Isles' location and weather can be a deterrent to many, and they are rarely very busy, even in peak season. The beauty of the location is that there is plenty of choice of places to explore, so even if the visitors' moorings at the islands' main ports of call are full, there are still plenty of anchorages to choose from, and many of these offer decent shelter.

THE WESTERN ISLES AT A GLANCE

Route length: Approximately 120nm.

Time required: Allow at least three weeks. If you intend to visit St Kilda, 42nm west of the Western Isles, allow longer.

When to go: May to September.

Weather: Changeable. Mild compared to Scotland's east coast, but conditions can deteriorate quickly, although visibility is generally good.

Type and size of boat: Power or sail, ideally of around 25–45ft (7.6–13.7m).

Equipment: Up-to-date charts, chartplotter, GPS, depth sounder, decent anchor, navigation lights, dependable engine.

Tides: Strong tidal streams prevail. Watch out for tides around exposed headlands too.

Hazards: Shallow waters, numerous rocks, strong tides. An uneven seabed in places can cause dangerous seas in bad weather.

Suitable for night sailing: Yes, with very careful pilotage and only in good weather. Many of the channels are now well marked, but up-to-date charts are essential.

Difficulty of route: Medium to hard.

Skills required: Excellent navigation and pilotage skills. Good boat handling. Anchoring knowledge.

Charts: Admiralty: SC 5616 (Scotland West Coast and Outer Hebrides): Imray: C66 (Mallaig to Rudha and Outer Hebrides), C67 (North Minch and Isle of Lewis), C68 (Cape Wrath to Wick and Isle of Lewis).

Berthing/mooring: There are 7 mooring options in the Western Isles: Castlebay on Barra has 12 moorings, Acarsaid Mhor on Eriskay has 2, Lochboisdale on South Uist has 6 (although new facilities are due to open in 2015), Lochmaddy on North Uist has 9 (more to open soon), while Berneray has 2 and Rodel on Harris has 3. The moorings are suitable for boats of a maximum 15 tonnes. A new 70-berth marina at Stornoway also has facilities for visiting yachts up to 78ft (24m) in length.

Ports of entry: Stornoway on Lewis is the largest port in the Western Isles.

Water: At Castlebay, Acarsaid Mhor, Lochboisdale, Lochmaddy, Berneray, Rodel and Stornoway.

Provisioning: Basic provisioning can be found at or near all the harbours, but Stornoway is your best option.

Fuel: At Castlebay, Acarsaid Mhor, Lochboisdale, Lochmaddy, Berneray, Rodel and Stornoway.

Shorepower: Available at Acarsaid Mhor, Lochboisdale, Berneray, Rodel and Stornoway.

Maintenance: At Stornoway.

Family friendliness: Yes, if you want beaches, historical sites and wildlife. No, if you are looking for theme parks and commercialized activities.

Further reading: *The Western Isles* by Martin Lawrence; *Outer Hebrides* by Clyde Cruising Club; *Cruising Scotland* by Mike Balmforth and Edward Mason.

left South Uist has plenty of historic interest such as traditional crofters' cottages.

VOYAGE 2

Norway

THE LOFOTEN AND VESTERÅLEN ISLANDS

The first thing that will strike you on approach by sea to the Lofoten Islands off Norway's northwest coast is the sheer scale of its 'Misty Mountains' – the soaring peaks of the Lofotenveggen or Lofoten Wall, which stretch for over 100km (60 miles) and appear to be almost totally impenetrable from halfway across the Vestfjorden. In fact, the granite mountain range is bisected by deep fjords and channels, which divide the Lofoten into six main islands and many more islets, and the Vesterålen, an archipelago that lies immediately to the northeast.

If you're looking for dramatic scenery, wild anchorages and seclusion, then the Lofoten and Vesterålen Islands are the place to come. Although popular with cruise ships and tourists from the mainland during the six weeks of the midnight sun, the islands have not yet become overrun with visiting yachts. Their location within the Arctic Circle and their fearsome reputation for stormy weather conditions deters many, yet those that do venture this far north will not be disappointed.

The islands, particularly to the south, teem with wildlife – the *nyker* or nesting cliffs are home to a vast array of seabirds – while the mountains offer superb walking and climbing, and the tiny fishing villages that line the eastern shores reveal a fascinating link with the cod industry in their 1,000 year-long history.

Although cruising in this area is totally weather dependent, and the more popular destinations can get busy with tourists, there are still many remote, secluded places to be found.

below Colourful houses dot the shoreline of the dramatic Lofoten Islands.

The route

Bodø in northwest Norway is the starting point of this cruise. It is north Norway's second biggest city and, as the gateway to the Lofoten and Vesterålen islands, can get very busy in peak season with tourists arriving by plane, train and cruise ship. As a place to stock up and start a voyage, however, it works well, and facilities for visiting yachtsmen are good.

From here, the nearest Lofoten Islands are an easy daysail away – around 44nm across the relatively protected waters of the Vestfjorden. The islands can be explored in any order, but by starting west of Bodø and working your way northeast up the island chain, you will get the opportunity to explore some of the quieter, less populated and more infrequently visited islands before encountering larger pockets of tourism at harbours such as Svolvær on the island of Austvågøya.

The first island of interest that you will reach is the low-lying Røst, the most southerly populated island in the archipelago. From there, continue northeast to Værøy, an island that contrasts greatly from Røst due to the soaring mountain that spans its length. Moskenesøya to the north offers the next possible anchorage, although extreme care must be taken in this area owing to the Mosktraumen – whirlpools and tidal eddies that are among the strongest in the world.

From Moskenesøya, continue northeast to the islands of Flakstadøya, Vestvågøya and then Austvågøya.

Although the narrows of Raftsundet, which lie between Austvågøya and Hinnøya, can have fast-running tidal streams of up to 7 knots, this is the main passage through to the Vesterålen islands, including Hadselgøya, Langøya and Andøya. You can return home to Bodø the way you came, or via a circular route that takes in the mainland coast to the north of your starting point, including anchorages at Sildpollen and Stefjordbotn.

below Forming a breathtaking backdrop, the Vesterålen Islands are the most northerly point on the cruise.

right Nusfjord is a traditional fishing village that has been preserved on the island of Flakstadøya.

Destinations

Whether it is picturesque historic harbour villages or remote and wild anchorages that you are after, you really are spoilt for choice within the Lofoten and Vesterålen islands.

Røst: This is the most southerly island in the chain that is inhabited and one of the most peaceful too. Less busy with tourists, it's a place to visit if you are interested in birdlife, and is said to produce the best air-dried cod in the archipelago. A selection of places to anchor can be found in the main harbour, but avoid anchoring here in poor weather conditions.

Værøy: Lying northeast of Røst, this island's name means 'weather' in Old Norse, and it can become an exposed place if conditions deteriorate. A fine-weather anchorage can be found off the beach at Sørland. Ashore you will find the oldest church in Lofoten, which has stood here since 1799, and several Viking burial sites. The seabird colonies are pretty impressive too.

Moskenesøya: The Lofoten and Vesterålen islands are characterized by their tiny fishing villages, which line many of the islands' east coasts. On Moskenesøya, the village of Å is delightful and home to two fishing museums – Tørrfiskmuseum and Norsk Fiskervaersmuseum – which give a fascinating insight into the fishing industry. The Vestfjorden, the area of sea that separates the Lofoten Islands from mainland Norway, is well known as the world's richest source of cod. Every January to April, millions of cod migrate here from the Barents Sea to spawn, and in the fishes' wake come the fishing boats, evidence of which can be found on most of the islands.

Flakstadøya: Another stunning island in the archipelago is Flakstadøya. Nusfjord is perhaps the best known place to visit – a traditional fishing village that has been 'preserved' and in which visitors can stay in *rorbuers*, or wooden fishermen's huts. Berths for visiting

yachts are available, or you could find berths at Sund which is to the west. Good anchorages can also be found at Straumøya.

Vestvågøya: One of the archipelago's most beautiful anchorages can be found on Vestvågøya, at Æsøya, and if the weather is good, then it is worth exploring. It is only very small, but stunning nonetheless. Alternatively, the harbours at Leknes, Stamsund and Ballstad usually have space for visiting yachts. Ballstad can be very busy with fishing boats, but there are good facilities here, including a boatyard and chandlery.

Austvågøya: This island is home to the capital of the Lofoten Islands – Svolvær. A sprawling town, Svolvær is also one of the most popular tourist destinations within the islands, and while the facilities and amenities ashore are very good, it can get very busy in peak season. Alternatively, Henningsvær, on the southwestern tip of the island, offers excellent facilities and plenty of room to berth. Grundfjorden on the island's northeast coast is a superb fine-weather anchorage.

Sildpollen and **Stefjordbotn:** Two destinations on the mainland coast are these remote and secluded anchorages. If the weather remains good both are a stunning place to spend the night.

Level of skill

This part of Norway is remote and relatively unpopulated, so visiting by boat means you need to be reasonably proficient in handling it and self-sufficient too. The climate here is mild, but Bodø is notoriously windy, so experience in heavy weather sailing is crucial as conditions can change rapidly.

The Lofoten Islands help to shelter the Vestfjorden – the area of water separating the archipelago from mainland Norway – from much of the Atlantic, but caution should be exercised when sailing among the islands, where squally conditions can prevail. In wind over tide conditions, the sea state can be particularly rough in these channels, many of which are rock-strewn and need careful pilotage throughout. In certain places, such as in the 13nm-long Raftsundet strait, which bisects the islands of Hinnøya and Austvågøya, tidal streams can be rapid, running at up to 7 knots.

The whirlpools of the Moskstraumen around Moskenesøya, Røst and Værøy, as immortalized in writing by Edgar Allan Poe and Jules Verne, should also be avoided, as the seas in this area can be particularly nasty.

Many of the harbours within the islands have alongside berths for visitors, albeit in small numbers, but anchoring skills are also essential if you want to explore the more remote side of the archipelago.

above Moskenesøya is home to many tiny fishing villages, but watch out for the off-lying whirlpools of Moskstraumen!

When to go

North Norway enjoys a subpolar oceanic climate, so despite this area being within the Arctic Circle, even the winters are fairly mild. The North Atlantic Drift is part of the reason for this, as it helps keep temperatures higher than in other countries within the Arctic Circle, and consequently you'll rarely see ice along this stretch of coast. However, Bodø is one of the windiest places in the whole of Norway, and the weather here can deteriorate quite rapidly, particularly in winter, when daylight hours are at a minimum too.

Most people tend to visit between May and August, when temperatures reach an average high of 16°C (61°F), and on occasion as much as 25°C (77°F). Time your visit mid-season, and you'll also experience the midnight sun, when 24-hour daylight dominates for a good six weeks.

Northwest Norway is still relatively quiet in terms of numbers of visiting cruising yachts, so despite its popularity with land-based tourists and cruise ships, it attracts far fewer boats than the south of the country. If you're looking for remote, secluded anchorages, then this area has plenty to offer.

THE LOFOTEN AND VESTERÅLEN ISLANDS AT A GLANCE

Route length: Approximately 200nm, depending on which islands you visit.

Time required: Allow at least a month. Two weeks would give you a whistle-stop tour, but with so many places to explore a month or more would give enough time to explore them more thoroughly.

When to go: May to August. From 2 June to 10 July this area experiences the midnight sun, when the sun is visible throughout the day and night.

Weather: Relatively mild considering this area lies within the Arctic Circle. July and August are the warmest months, with average high temperatures near Bodø reaching around 16°C (61°F). April, May and June are the driest months, but July and August can be wet. There can be strong winds, too, with Bodø being the windiest city in north Norway.

Type and size of boat: Power or sail, ideally of around 35–55ft (10.7–16.8m).

Equipment: Up-to-date charts, chartplotter, GPS, depth sounder, decent anchor, dependable engine.

Tides: High water in the Vestfjorden area is 1½ hours after High Water Bergen. Tidal streams can be fast, running at around 4 knots in between some of the bigger Lofoten Islands, while in the narrows at Raftsundet, 7 knots is not unusual.

Hazards: Strong winds, numerous rocks and islets, lumpy seas in wind over tide conditions, fast-running tidal streams between the islands.

Suitable for night sailing: Yes, as during the summer months, and particularly June and July, there are very few hours of darkness.

Difficulty of route: Medium to hard.

Skills required: Excellent navigation and pilotage skills, good boat handling and the ability to anchor.

Charts: The best charts of this area are provided by the Norwegian Hydrographic Service. Its Main Chart Series covers the area in great detail, at a scale of 1:50,000. For more detailed charts on particular ports, see its Harbour Chart Series: 476 (Bodø), 462 (Svolvaer). For an overview of the area, see its Coastal Chart Series: 311 (Fra Støtt til Andenes). The Admiralty chart 2328 covers the Lofoten Islands to Vesterålen.

Berthing/mooring: Visitors' berths can be found in harbours throughout the area. Bodø has a marina, but numerous harbours within the Lofoten Islands, including Ballstad and Leknes on Vestvågøya and Henningsvær and Svolvær on Austvågøya, also offer overnight berths for visitors.

Ports of entry: Bodø.

Water: Available at most harbours on the mainland and Lofoten Islands.

Provisioning: Basic provisioning available at most harbours, but if you need to stock up, do so at Bodø.

Fuel: Widely available, including at Bodø, Ballstad and Leknes on Vestvågoya and Svolvaer and Henningsvær on Austvagøya.

Shorepower: At Bodø and numerous ports within the Lofoten Islands.

Maintenance: At Bodø and throughout the Lofoten Islands, including Ballstad on Vestvågøya.

Family friendliness: Bodø offers many attractions, but the islands are remote and uncommercialized.

Further reading: *Norway* by Judy Lomax (RCC Pilotage Foundation); *Norwegian Cruising Guide* by Phyllis L Nickel and John H Harries; *Norwegian Cruising Guide* by John Armitage and Mark Brackenbury.

VOYAGE 3

Sweden

THE STOCKHOLM ARCHIPELAGO

With 30,000 islands and skerries to choose from, you are not short of places to visit within the Stockholm Archipelago, or skärgården as it is known locally. The area is thickly peppered with rocky outcrops. Some of these are inhabited, others are not, which helps create a sailing destination of great distinction. The Stockholm Archipelago is stunningly beautiful, and although the sailing can at times be challenging, it is also some of the finest in northern Europe.

The archipelago, as it looks today, dates to the Viking Age (793 to 1066CE) and extends eastwards from Stockholm for around 50nm into the Baltic Sea. Its southernmost extremity is marked by the island of Oja, to the south of the mainland port of Nynäshamn, while its northernmost point is Väddö, the seventh largest island, in the northernmost district of Norrtälje.

The islands cater well for visiting yachtsmen. Boating is big business here, and during the peak summer months thousands of people sail these islands. However, the beauty of this area is that with so many destinations and an infinite number of routes, it is not hard to escape the crowds. Many of the larger islands are inhabited, with an estimated 50,000 holiday homes scattered throughout the archipelago, while others are quieter, offering peaceful anchorages in the wilderness.

If it is city life that you wish to explore, the final destination of Stockholm – the Venice of the North – is hard to beat. Home to a multitude of shops, restaurants and cultural sites, the city welcomes visiting boats with open arms.

below It is not hard to find quiet spots to enjoy the beauty and wilderness of this region.

The route

Choosing a specific route through the Stockholm Archipelago is tricky. There are so many islands and skerries to choose from and so many alternative ways to get there, that to describe a definite route through the area would be to deny you the chance to explore the archipelago to its full potential. However, there are certain destinations that should not be missed, and the route outlined below, which follows a linear path, takes you on a tour of some of the best.

The starting destination is Nynäshamn, which lies about 35nm southwest of Stockholm on the mainland coast. From here, it is a short 10nm hop to the island of Utö, before the route continues northeast to Sandhamn, passing the islands of Ornö and Nämdö en route.

Continue north for about 10nm and you will reach the island of Möja, before heading north-northwest to Finnhamn. From here, sail north-northeast to Blidö, before bearing away to the southwest and heading to Grinda, some 19nm away. It is then a 15nm passage eastwards to Vaxholm before the route concludes in Stockholm.

To extend the cruise further, you could continue northeast of Finnhamn to Åland (see page 26) and its satellite islands, which lie 70nm to the northeast of Stockholm across a stretch of water – the South Kvarken.

below Stockholm is the end point of this cruise and has excellent facilities and heritage.

Destinations

Nynäshamn: The former spa town of Nynäshamn lies to the south of Stockholm on the mainland, and in 1912 hosted the sailing events of the Olympic Games. Today it is a busy town with a large marina and can get quite crowded during peak season. The facilities ashore are very good, with a wide choice of excellent restaurants and cafés. The off-lying island of Bedarön offers several alternative anchorages on its east coast and is well protected from the prevailing winds.

Sandhamn: For over 200 years this island has been a popular destination with sailors, especially for yacht racing. The Royal Swedish Yacht Club is based here, and it is the start location of several famous yacht races, including the ÅF Offshore Race. Ashore, the village of Sandhamn is surprisingly modest, with only around 100 permanent residents, and as a result it has suffered only minimal commercialization. There is a good marina here and at the neighbouring island of Lökholmen.

Finnhamn: Lying in the centre of the archipelago, Finnhamn is a popular destination with boats travelling to and from Stockholm. It is named after the Finnish ships that once used the harbour. There are several places to berth on the island, but the best by far, and also the most popular at peak season, is at Paradiset on the west coast. Once through the narrow entrance the pool offers good all-round shelter and links ashore.

Grinda: The inner and outer archipelagos are easy to distinguish for their terrain. In comparison to the outer islands, the inner ones are lush and verdant and Grinda is no exception. The harbour is located on the northwest side of the island and offers a good range of marina facilities, including space for 100 boats, fuel, shorepower, showers and toilets. Ashore there is a large Jugendstil-style house designed by Ernst Stenhammar, which is now an inn.

Vaxholm: Built in 1548 the fortress on the islet of Vaxholmen, which lies next to Vaxholm, gave this island its name. Standing guard on the approach to Vaxholm, it is now a museum and an interesting place to visit. The town itself was a spa town in the 1880s, and today there is a harbour with berths for around 100 visiting boats, and good facilities.

Stockholm: If you can, leave plenty of time to explore Stockholm when you are cruising this area. Although the archipelago offers extensive destinations and opportunities for solitude, Stockholm is a beautiful city and worthy of a longer stay. With over 100 museums, good shopping and excellent dining facilities, it has something for everyone, and during the summer it becomes a hub of activity. The city itself is built on 14 islands, which lie at the entrance to Lake Mälaren. Stockholm is home to an excellent range of facilities for boats, including 14 marinas. One museum that should not be missed is the Vasamuseet, home to the Swedish warship *Vasa*, which was built in 1626 and sank on her maiden voyage. Salvaged and largely intact, she is an incredible sight.

Level of skill

Sailing within the Stockholm Archipelago requires considerable experience, and it is not an area for the novice sailor. As you might expect, rocks pose the biggest hazard here. Most of the area is well charted, and because of the complexity of the sailing ground it is well worth investing in a set of large-scale charts to navigate by. However, many of the skerries and rocks are unmarked and unbuoyed, so it is crucial that you keep a record of your progress when navigating through the archipelago, especially if you are not following a standard route.

Most pilot guides rate eyeball navigation over electronics, particularly as some of the channels between the islands run within metres of the rocks' edges. Depths can be challenging too, as in some areas deep water can shoal very quickly, so check your charts and keep a close eye on the depth sounder.

Another big hazard is other boats. During the summer months this area is alive with on-the-water activity, and consequently some anchorages and harbours can become very crowded and congested. To avoid the crowds, keep away from the standard routes if you are confident about navigation. This area is also heavy with ferry traffic heading into and away from Stockholm. Ferries have right of way at all times, and even in a situation where the channel is wide enough to allow you to pass safely alongside, you must give way and wait until the passage is clear. Watch out for the ferries' wash too.

The tidal range within the Stockholm Archipelago is minimal, although you may come across fast-flowing currents in some of the narrower channels. The outer islands are also rather exposed to the Baltic Sea, affording little shelter, so it is important to keep an eye on the forecasts. Even in the inner archipelago, the wind can be problematic, with squally conditions and short seas appearing with little warning. It is important to have contingency plans if you need to run for shelter, particularly as not all anchorages and harbours offer all-round protection.

When to go

Sweden enjoys a temperate climate, with cold winters and warm summers. During the summer months, temperatures average 20–25°C (68–77°F), but can rise up to 30°C (86°F), and during July and August it is not unusual to see 17–18°C (62–64°F) at night. The sailing season is relatively short, running from early June to late September, but early in the season Stockholm's northerly location means that daylight hours are very long, with sunrise at around 3.40am and sunset as late as 10pm, so you have plenty of time to explore.

Most local people take to their boats during August, so expect the archipelago to be busy then. Later in the season it is quieter, but the weather is usually fair, so you can continue sailing until the end of September.

During the summer months wind conditions within the archipelago are generally light, although localized squally conditions can whip up quickly. The prevailing winds are from the southwest.

THE STOCKHOLM ARCHIPELAGO AT A GLANCE

Route length: Around 150nm, depending on which route through the islands you take.

Time required: One month would allow a good amount of time for a thorough exploration of this area. Two weeks would give you an overview.

When to go: June to September.

Weather: A temperate climate with warm summers and cold winters. July is the hottest month. The prevailing winds are from the southwest.

Type and size of boat: Power or sail, 25ft (7.6m) plus.

Equipment: A good set of large-scale charts, binoculars, depth sounder, anchor.

Tides: Minimal. Tidal currents through some of the narrow channels can be fast running.

Hazards: Rocks, ferries and other leisure craft, squally conditions.

Suitable for night sailing: No.

Difficulty of route: Moderate to hard.

Skills required: Excellent ability to navigate through crowded, rocky waters and the ability to anchor.

Charts: Admiralty: 811 (Port of Stockholm), 820 (Sweden East Coast – Stockholm's Skargard, Vastra Saxafjarden to Stockholm), 821 (Stockholm's Skargard, Sandhamn to Ostra Saxarf Jarden), 831 (Stockholm's Skargard Namdof Jarden), 836 (Stockholm's Skargard; Mysingen to Jungfrufjarden), 881 (Outer Approaches to Sandhamn), 832 (Stockholm's Skargard, approaches to Sandhamn), 2362 (Approaches to Stockholm), 872 (Stockholm's Skargard Nynashamn to Dalaro). Delius Klasing: Satz 12 (Ostkste Schweden 2).

Berthing/mooring: There are numerous harbours offering alongside, bow- or stern-to berthing throughout the archipelago. There are marinas at Nynäshamn, Stockholm, Grinda and Sandhamn. There is also a wide choice of anchorages; anchor off with stern or bowline taken ashore.

Ports of entry: Stockholm, Sandhamn and Nynäshamn.

Water: Widely available at a range of marinas and harbours.

Provisioning: Widely available. Nynäshamn and Stockholm offer the most extensive choice, but smaller harbours and towns are usually well stocked.

Fuel: Widely available at marinas and harbours.

Shorepower: Widely available at marinas and harbours.

Maintenance: This area is well set up for boats, so there is plenty of choice when it comes to boatyard repair and engineering facilities.

Family friendliness: Very family friendly.

Further reading: *The Baltic Sea* by RCC Pilotage Foundation.

left The lush foliage of Grinda is typical of the inner islands of the archipelago.

VOYAGE 4

Finland

THE ÅLAND ARCHIPELAGO AND HELSINKI

There are said to be over 180,000 islands off Finland's Baltic coast. These waters, which stretch from the northeastern corner of the Gulf of Bothnia to Hamina and the border with Russia, are so densely populated with islands that some people have joked that it is possible to walk from the Åland Islands (the country's westernmost extremity, 70nm northeast of Stockholm in Sweden) to Helsinki on the Finnish mainland without even touching the water.

For sailors this forms the basis of an incredible cruising ground, one with infinite possibilities of places to visit and explore, some of them off the beaten track. You're spoilt for choice for places to anchor as there are literally thousands of sheltered anchorages to be found off the coast. The beauty of this place is that if one bay or inlet is too busy, it is only a short hop before you find another. While only some of the islands have amenities, the mainland coast has over 200 harbours and marinas to choose from, most of which welcome visiting boats.

The scenery here is simply stunning. Finland has the largest area of forest in Europe and much of the coastline is densely forested. Other parts, including many of the outlying islands, are more barren, with sparse vegetation punctuated by distinctive and brightly coloured fishermen's houses. It is an area that is rich in rural rugged beauty, where nature and its wildlife thrive. Although the prospect of navigating through the myriad inter-island channels may be daunting to the first-time visitor, it is well worth the effort.

below There are myriad unspoilt islands to visit in the Åland Archipelago.

The route

This cruise follows one of the more traditional routes through Finland, starting at the Åland Islands in the west, before exploring the southern part of the Turku Archipelago and then the Finnish mainland before arriving at Helsinki, the final destination. The route is around 170nm, but it is very easy to make it longer, either by stopping off at more islands along the way, or by exploring more of the Turku Archipelago, which lies to the east of the Åland Islands. For those wishing to explore even farther afield, St Petersburg in Russia is a worthy destination, 150nm to the east.

The starting point on this cruise, the Åland Islands, are 70nm northeast of Stockholm in Sweden. The biggest town here is Mariehamn (Maarianhamina), and this is a good place for setting off. From here, follow the buoyed channels south-southeast to the island of Rödhamn, before continuing east to Kökar. The route continues east to the island of Jurmo. Nötö, to the northeast, is the next destination, and then Gullkrona, before the route meanders in a southeasterly direction to Hankö on the mainland coast. This first part of the route is just over 100nm in length.

The next part of the cruise visits Tammisaari (Ekenäs), before continuing eastwards to the final destination at Helsinki, 70nm east of Hankö.

below Boats are a part of life here so there are plenty of good moorings along the route.

Destinations

Åland Islands: No cruise is complete without exploring the Åland Islands. The archipelago is an autonomous region of Finland, which comprises 6,500 islands and skerries, and lies at the southern end of the Gulf of Bothnia. Its population is largely Swedish speaking and many of the islands have Swedish and Finnish names. There are an infinite number of destinations within the islands, and Åland itself, the main island in the archipelago, has several places of interest including Mariehamn (Maarianhamina), the island's main town. There are two marinas here, the Västerhamn on the western side of the town and the Österhamn on the eastern side. Both welcome visitors, although the former is quieter than the latter. Österhamn is larger and more popular with the locals, but it does offer more shelter in southwesterly winds. Ashore you'll find excellent amenities, shops, bars and restaurants. Other sites to visit on Åland include the medieval Kastelholm Castle on the eastern coast of the island, which can be visited via the conveniently located marina nearby, as well as delightful anchorages to the east at Bomarsund and on the northern coast at Geta Djupviken.

Rödhamn: Lying 10nm south of Mariehamn, the island of Rödhamn is a popular first port of call for boats heading east. The island was once used by Baltic traders sheltering from bad weather en route to and from Sweden, and the harbour offers good shelter from nearly all directions. Facilities are minimal, but the freshly baked bread, wood-burning sauna and museum make it worth a visit.

Kökar: Directly east of Rödhamn is Kökar, which comprises three islands. These are Karlby, Finnö and Helsö, each of which has a marina. Karlby marina has a tricky approach, but Sandvik and Helsö marinas are easier and offer good all-round shelter.

Jurmo: One of the outlying islands in the Turku Archipelago, Jurmo is well known for its Bronze Age stone circles. The 5km (3 mile) long island is an idyllic place to stop, and has a marina on its northwestern coast with berths for up to 80 boats, although it can get busy during peak season.

Nötö: An alternative to Jurmo is the island of Nötö, which lies to the north-northeast. Here you'll find a small marina on the southwestern coast, several anchorages and basic amenities.

Gullkrona: Lying to the northeast of Nötö, Gullkrona is a delightful place to visit. It's a private island so boats are not permitted to overnight here, but ashore there is a small shop and museum, as well as good walks.

Hankö: The first mainland port on this cruise lies 100nm east of Mariehamn. Its East Harbour has two marinas that offer good facilities, and as a popular destination with visiting yachts, it can get very busy in peak season. It also has a good shopping centre close by.

Tammisaari (Ekenäs): Sail 10nm east of Hankö and you will arrive at Tammisaari. The 12nm approach channel winds through the islands but is clearly buoyed. On arrival you will find a pretty town, a good beach and berths for visiting boats.

Helsinki: The final destination on this route is Finland's capital city and the country's yachting centre. You can tell this not only by the number of boats, but the sheer number of marinas and yachting facilities within the city and surrounding area – 15 at the last count. If you need something for the boat, or you need something fixed, this is the place in Finland to come, but it is also a fascinating place to explore on foot. The shops and markets are excellent and anyone with an interest in cathedrals will be spoilt for choice.

Level of skill

The primary hazard on this route is rocks. The sheer number of skerries and islands within this cruising area is quite daunting, so those that attempt it should be skilled at reading charts. This is, however, a popular cruising destination used by thousands of boats each year, so most of the main channels are well marked.

It's important to keep a close eye on your chart and depth sounder. Some of the channels are very deep, but surprisingly narrow too, requiring you to pass within a stone's toss of the rocks. Owing to the vast number of skerries and islands in this area, most of which are indistinguishable from each other, it is easy to get lost!

Take great care on approach to some of the larger harbours such as Mariehamn, where the approach channel is very narrow. This channel is regularly used by large ferries travelling from Helsinki and Sweden and they have priority over all other boats.

Another skill that is required is the ability to anchor. Although you could quite happily travel from one marina or harbour quayside to another on this route, if you are able to anchor you will be able to explore more secluded destinations. The tides here are negligible, and

above Rocks are the chief hazard but the main channels are deep and well marked.

there are plenty of anchorages to choose from. You can usually anchor in depths of 2–5m on mud. Techniques for anchoring in the Baltic differ from elsewhere in Europe in that the anchor is usually dropped from the stern, with a bowline taken ashore onto a rock or tree.

When to go

Finland has a subarctic, or boreal, climate. Warmed by the Gulf Stream, temperatures in the summer reach an average of 17°C (62°F) with highs of 23°C (73°C), and up to 20 hours of sunlight. However, during the winter months temperatures can drop as low as -20°C (-4°F).

The sailing season in Finland is surprisingly short, and runs from May to September. Most local boats sail only in June and July. The sailing in September is still good, although you may not find all the facilities you require as easily. The advantage of this though is that it is quieter.

THE ÅLAND ARCHIPELAGO AND HELSINKI AT A GLANCE

Route length: Around 170nm depending on how many islands or harbours you visit.

Time required: Two weeks minimum.

When to go: May to September.

Weather: Warm summers, with average temperatures of 17°C (62°F); cold winters when temperatures can fall as low as -20°C (-4°F).

Type and size of boat: No restriction on type or size. Many of the islands are such short distances away that dayboats and dinghies are as suitable as yachts to explore these waters.

Equipment: A good set of charts, chartplotter, depth sounder, anchor, long lines to take ashore, reliable engine.

Tides: Small enough not to be a concern.

Hazards: Lots of rocks, ferries and plenty of inter-island traffic.

Suitable for night sailing: No. This area is littered with so many rocks, islets and skerries, many of which are unmarked and unlit, that cruising around in this area at night is not advised.

Difficulty of route: Moderate to hard.

Skills required: Good navigation and pilotage skills, and the ability to anchor.

Charts: Admiralty: 2297 (Saaristomeri and Ålands Hav), 3437 (Hanka, Maarianhamina, Parainen, Paraisten Portti and Uusikaupunki), 3439 (Outer Approaches to Turku), 3443 (Approaches to Hanko), 2241 (Entrance to Gulf of Finland), 2248 (Gulf of Finland – Western Part), 2218 (Helsinki), 3818 (Approaches to Helsinki).

Berthing/mooring: A huge amount of choice. There are marinas and yacht harbours or quays of varying sizes on most of the islands and mainland ports with bow- or stern-to mooring. There are plenty of sheltered anchorages to choose from too.

Ports of entry: Mariehamn on Åland, Suomenlinna Island near Helsinki.

Water: Available at most ports and marinas.

Provisioning: A huge amount of choice. Most of the mainland towns and harbours have good shopping centres and the basics at the very least can be found on the larger islands.

Fuel: Available at most ports and marinas.

Shorepower: Available at most ports and marinas.

Maintenance: This area caters well for cruising boats, and most of the marinas and ports offer some boatyard maintenance services. The close proximity of all the harbours means that if you can't find the service you require in one port, you should be able to in another nearby.

Family friendliness: Very family friendly. Lots of places to explore ashore and short distances between the islands means that boredom on board doesn't need to last long! Helsinki has lots of family friendly attractions too.

Further reading: *The Baltic Sea* by RCC Pilotage Foundation.

VOYAGE 5

England

THE ISLES OF SCILLY

Characterized by its crystal-clear, azure-coloured waters, bleached white, super-fine sandy beaches and palm trees, the Isles of Scilly would not look out of place in the Caribbean. Yet this archipelago of around 140 islands and rocky outcrops lies just 24nm west-southwest of Land's End, the southernmost tip of mainland Britain.

Once thought to have been one big island known as Ennor, but long since subsumed by rising sea levels caused by glacial melt waters of the last Ice Age, the archipelago now comprises numerous islands, islets and rocks that cover around 130sq km (50 square miles). Of the larger islands, only five are inhabited – St Mary's, Tresco, St Martin's, Bryher and St Agnes – and these are home to a population of just 2,200.

As a cruising destination, the Isles of Scilly are hard to beat. Tranquil waters, excellent birdwatching, perfect beaches and historic sites all within close proximity provide plenty for visitors to do. Its mild climate is a big attraction too, and although the islands can become inundated with tourists during peak season, it is still possible to find secluded parts and quiet anchorages.

However, it is also a cruising area that should not be taken lightly. Anyone venturing into these waters should do so with extreme caution, as the archipelago lies in a particularly exposed part of the Atlantic – one that should only be explored in settled conditions owing to the infinite number of unmarked rocks and reefs and strong tidal streams. In the right conditions, though, the Isles of Scilly are a gem of a place and arguably one of the top ten places to explore in Europe.

below In settled conditions, the Isles of Scilly are one of the most tranquil destinations in Europe.

The route

Although this is a circular route around the Isles of Scilly, it is easiest to start off from the English mainland. There are excellent transport links between Hugh Town on St Mary's and Penzance. Falmouth, which is 34nm to the east of Penzance, is a more preferable option though. The distance to the Isles of Scilly is greater – 65nm as opposed to 35nm from Penzance – but the facilities at Falmouth are arguably better, with the option of numerous marinas and visitors' moorings, boat repair and maintenance amenities, chandlers and plenty of places to restock and recharge, particularly as there are no marina facilities within the Scilly Isles. Falmouth is also a good place to hide if the weather turns nasty.

Once clear of The Manacles – a notorious cluster of half-tide rocks southeast of the entrance to Falmouth Harbour – make sure you time your passage accurately, so as to catch a fair tide around the Lizard and across Mount's Bay. From there, head on a bearing for Peninnis Head, the southernmost headland on St Mary's, which marks the entrance to St Mary's Sound, between the islands of St Mary's and St Agnes and Gugh. The area to the west of the Wolf Rock Lighthouse is part of the Land's End Traffic Separation Scheme, which should be crossed at right angles and a good lookout maintained.

The Isles of Scilly are low-lying, and even in good visibility can be tricky to identify until close in. A red and white horizontally striped daymark on a headland identifies the northeast corner of St Martin's, however. Once you have identified the islands, St Mary's Harbour can be approached via either St Mary's Sound or Crow Sound to the northeast. From there you are in close proximity to St Agnes, Gugh, Samson, Tresco and St Martin's.

below Offering rural and unspoilt charm, St Agnes and Gugh join together at Low Water.

Destinations

The five main islands are the places to visit in the Isles of Scilly, each of which has its own individual character.

St Mary's: This is the capital of the Isles of Scilly, and the largest of the five main islands. Home to around 1,600 people, the key focus of the island is Hugh Town, which as well as providing the majority of the boat-related facilities and services within the islands is the drop-off point for visitors arriving via the RMS *Scillonian III* from Penzance. Here you'll find a number of visitors' moorings in St Mary's Pool, and the widest range of shops in the archipelago. For anyone interested in ancient history the island has much to offer in the form of the Halangy Down Ancient Village and Bant's Carn Burial Chamber, while its white-sand beaches and 48km (30 miles) of coastal paths provide good opportunities to stretch your legs.

St Agnes: Lying to the southwest of St Mary's, St Agnes and its neighbouring islet Gugh, which are joined together at Low Water, are the least developed of the archipelago, with the lowest number of permanent inhabitants. It has a lovely rural charm about it, and much of its interior is taken up with flower fields serving the islands' thriving cut-flower industry. Stunning beaches and good anchorages – particularly in westerly winds – can also be found.

Bryher: Just 2km (1.2 miles) long by 1km (0.6 miles) wide, Bryher is the smallest of the main islands, and lies to the west of Tresco. Idyllic white-sand beaches on the southern side contrast heavily with the rugged northern coast, but the island also offers several good anchorages, including the drying Green Bay, which is suitable for shoal-draught boats. There are also three Sites of Special Scientific Interest (SSSIs) on the island.

Tresco: If you are looking for a protected anchorage, then New Grimsby Sound, between Tresco and Bryher, offers the most shelter in the archipelago. Home to over 20 visitors' moorings, as well as a good anchorage, it can

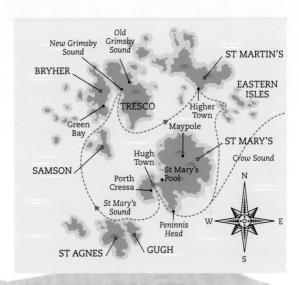

be very crowded in peak season, but is close to some delightfully secluded beaches and a good place from which to visit the famous Tresco Abbey Gardens and Tregarthen Hill Bronze Age tomb. The island itself is privately owned, but it is very welcoming to any visiting yachtsmen.

St Martin's: With its distinctive red and white striped daymark, St Martin's is often the first island that is identified on approach to the archipelago. Less popular with visitors, it nonetheless boasts some of the most beautiful and unspoilt beaches in the UK, and for visiting yachtsmen there are several anchorages suitable for boats of moderate draught. Ashore, you'll find a vineyard, plus several art galleries, as well as basic supplies.

Other islands: Inhabited until the 1850s, Samson's residents are now just black rabbits, although the remains of the former farmers' cottages can still be seen. Bar Point on its northeast shore offers a small anchorage from which to explore. The Eastern Isles – a group of 12 islets that lie to the east of St Martin's and St Mary's – can also be visited, but are only recommended in very settled weather.

Level of skill

The Isles of Scilly can be a tricky area to sail, with many hazards, and consequently a high level of skill and boat handling experience is required. The islands lie in a very exposed area of the Atlantic, and so changes in the weather can be rapid. In good weather, the islands can be a delightful place, but when the weather turns, they offer few places of refuge, and crossings to or from the mainland should not be attempted. Gale-force winds are common too, particularly in the winter months, which, when combined with poor visibility and Atlantic swell, can make this area an unpleasant place. A good understanding of the weather and an ability to read synoptic charts is therefore essential.

Good knowledge of pilotage and navigation is also a must, as well as the ability to read a chart, as not only are there off-lying hazards such as The Manacles, Wolf Rock and shipping within the Land's End Traffic Separation Zone en route from Falmouth, but the tidal streams around the islands are often erratic and fast-running, depending on the state of the tide. A vast number of rocks and shallows in the waters surrounding the islands mean that particular care must be taken on approach, and even within the islands a good lookout should be maintained at all times. However, the clear waters do make it possible to spot many of the below-the-water hazards in settled conditions.

Anyone attempting this cruise should also be experienced at boat handling in close quarters. In peak season, many of the anchorages and areas of visitors' moorings become very crowded, so you need to be experienced at manoeuvring in tight spaces. A good working knowledge of laying your anchor securely is also crucial, particularly if inclement weather comes in while you are there. Not all anchorages and moorings are suitable in all weathers, so be prepared to move if necessary and research the area in enough detail so that you know safer places to retreat to. Tidal range within the islands can be as much as 6m at Springs, so bear this in mind when anchoring too.

When to go

May to September or October is the time to visit the Isles of Scilly. The Romans nicknamed them the 'Sun Isles', and it is not hard to see why, as during the summer months this area enjoys plenty of sunshine. Compared with the rest of the UK, the Isles of Scilly have a very mild climate, with temperatures in the peak season being on average around 19–20°C (66–68°F). Transport links to the mainland are good, and consequently the islands are very popular with visitors during the summer, with tourism now accounting for 85 per cent of all income to the local economy.

During August, the islands are also a popular destination with French sailors, and so visitors' moorings and the numerous anchorages around the islands can become busy, and in places very crowded. If you are looking for secluded anchorages and beaches, then arrive earlier in the season when fewer people visit but when the temperatures are still mild.

THE ISLES OF SCILLY AT A GLANCE

Route length: Approximately 65nm, depending on which islands you visit.

Time required: A week to 10 days would give a brief introduction to the main islands, but if you want to explore them further, then allow at least two weeks.

When to go: May to September/October, although June and July are the best.

Weather: Mild compared to the rest of the UK, but owing to its exposed location expect rapid changes in the weather. Gales are common in winter.

Type and size of boat: Power or sail, ideally of around 25–45ft (7.6–13.7m). Strong tidal streams mean that plenty of sail or engine power is essential. Anchorages/moorings get very busy, so space for big boats is limited.

Equipment: Up-to-date charts, chartplotter, GPS, depth sounder, good anchor, a dependable engine.

Tides: At times erratic, and often strong. Be wary of tidal streams close in.

Hazards: Shipping, strong and often tricky tidal races, unmarked and unlit rocks, reefs, shallow water and pot buoys.

Suitable for night sailing: Definitely not – too many rocks, shallow reefs and challenging tides.

Difficulty of route: Hard.

Skills required: Excellent navigation and pilotage skills, good boat handling and plenty of experience of anchoring are essential.

Charts: Admiralty: 34 (Isles of Scilly), 1148 (Isles of Scilly to Land's End), 2565 (St Agnes Head to Dodman Point including the Isles of Scilly), SC5603 (Falmouth to Padstow, including Isles of Scilly), C7 (Falmouth to Isles of Scilly). Imray: 2400.2 (Approaches to the Isles of Scilly), 2400.3 (Isles of Scilly).

Berthing/mooring: Limited. Visitors' moorings in New Grimsby Sound and Old Grimsby Sound, St Mary's Pool and Porth Cressa, but apart from three drying berths in St Mary's Harbour, there are no other alongside berths or marinas. Numerous anchorages, but many are weather dependent.

Ports of entry: As preferred, as there is no Customs office on the islands.

Water: Limited supply, so fill up in Falmouth.

Provisioning: Most supplies can be obtained, but prices are expensive in comparison to the mainland as many things are imported.

Fuel: On St Mary's only.

Shorepower: Available only at the drying berths in St Mary's Harbour.

Maintenance: Boat repair services, marine engineers and chandlers on St Mary's.

Family friendliness: Facilities are limited, but the beaches and islands are well geared for tourists.

Further reading: *Isles of Scilly Pilot* by Graham Adam; *NP255 Tidal Stream Atlas – Falmouth to Padstow (including the Isles of Scilly); The West Country Cruising Companion (8th Edition)* by Mark Fishwick.

left Although weather conditions can be tricky, there are plenty of sheltered anchorages available.

VOYAGE 6

France

THE INLAND WATERWAYS

If you're planning to sail to the Mediterranean from northern Europe, but don't have the time or inclination to go 'round the outside' via the Atlantic coasts of France, Spain and Portugal, then consider taking the inland route. With 4,345nm of navigable inland waterways, it is possible to travel from the English Channel to the Mediterranean in just one month, experiencing some wonderful parts of the country en route.

Many people use the inland route purely as a means of getting from A to B in the quickest possible time, but as a cruising destination France's inland waterways have lots to offer, including infinite variety. If you want to explore major cities, you can, as many of the routes south pass through Paris, Chalon-sur-Saône and Lyon. If you're looking for rural tranquillity, you'll find that too, as well as a pleasing number of towns and villages within easy reach of the canal and riverbanks.

Moorings for the night are also widespread and varied. Many towns and villages along the canals have quays where visitors can lie alongside, while in more major towns and cities, marinas provide a wider choice of facilities. At the latter, you can expect to pay berthing prices comparable to most other marinas in France, but in the more rural locations, overnight fees can be very reasonable indeed.

Foundations for the canal networks were first constructed in the 1500s, and although the waterways' heyday was in the 19th century, they remain very popular with tourists and boatowners.

below At Chalon-sur-Saône, calm waters make this a perfect place for a stopover.

The route

From the English Channel there are several options for entry into the inland waterway network for routes heading to the Mediterranean. One of the most popular is via the port of Le Havre, travelling up the tidal River Seine to Rouen for around 52nm before joining the non-tidal canal network and proceeding southeasterly to Paris, a farther 61nm away.

From just south of Paris there is the option of two routes to the next major port of call, Chalon-sur-Saône. You can either head southeast via Haute-Seine, Canal du Loing, Canal de Briare, Canal latéral à la Loire and Canal du Centre, or east along the River Marne, Canal latéral à la Marne, Canal entre Champagne et Bourgogne and the River Saône. The easterly route is around 26nm longer than the southeasterly route at 304nm, while the southeasterly route has more locks. However, if you are interested in visiting the Palace of Fontainebleau, then the southeasterly route goes right past it.

At Chalon-sur-Saône the routes converge on the River Saône, before heading onto the River Rhône. From there it is another 217nm to Arles. From Arles, it is just 44nm to the coast at Grau du Roi, or you can head farther along the coast to Sète, 70nm to the west. In total, the whole route from Le Havre to Sète is about 695nm.

below The Palace of Fontainebleau lies just outside Paris and is easy to visit on your journey south.

Destinations

The number of places to visit en route from Le Havre to Sète is huge, and you really are spoilt for choice. Many of the places you will pass are just small and fairly isolated villages, whereas others are major cities, and it can be a real treat to arrive there by water.

Rouen: The first big city you come to after Le Havre is Rouen. Famous for its historic cathedral and castle, it is a fascinating place to explore if you have an interest in art, history or sporting events.

Paris: If there is one way to arrive in the heart of France's capital it's by boat. Arriving via the River Seine is an incredible way to see the sights. Expect heavy river traffic, however, particularly near the centre. The Arsenal Port La Bastille marina is on the Saint Martin Canal, located near Île Saint-Louis, and although visitors' berths (available up to 82ft/25m in length) are expensive, you won't find a better place to stop if you want to explore the city. Alternatively the smaller La Villette marina, which can accommodate boats up to 49ft (15m) in length, is just slightly farther to the north.

Palace of Fontainebleau: The royal Palace of Fontainebleau is another magnificent destination. Lying 55km (35 miles) outside Paris, it is possible to visit the palace en route south, as the Canal du Loing passes to the south of it. Set in huge parkland, it's an impressive palace, with a fascinating history.

Épernay: Situated on the banks of the River Marne, Épernay is at the heart of champagne country, and an interesting place to visit if you want to sample some of the world's finest bubbly.

Briare Aqueduct: Until 2003 this was the longest navigable aqueduct in the world. Spanning the River Loire at Châtillon-sur-Loire, the 662m (2,172ft) aqueduct carries the Canal lateral à la Loire across 15 arches. It's a magnificent structure to cross, and dates back to 1896. Part of the construction of the aqueduct was overseen

by Gustave Eiffel, in the year before work was started on the Eiffel Tower.

Chalon-sur-Saône: The midway point of this cruise is Chalon-sur-Saône, a former naval base that stands on the banks of the River Saône. Offering all the attractions of a major town, Chalon-sur-Saône is the birthplace of Joseph Nicéphore Niépce, who is credited with inventing photography. A museum to honour him, plus numerous art galleries, museums, cafés and restaurants make this an interesting place to stop off.

Arles: Julius Caesar held Arles in great respect during his reign, and his influence is apparent throughout the city. A 20,000-seat amphitheatre, still used today for controversial bullfights, forms the main focus of visitors' attention, but anyone interested in art is also in for a treat. Vincent Van Gogh lived here between 1888 and 1889, and many of the landscapes he painted were based on the area.

Sète: This final destination lies on the Mediterranean coast. It's a very traditional port, unspoilt by tourism, and a great place to be introduced to Mediterranean life, with beautiful beaches, an intriguing network of canals and plenty of good food available.

Level of skill

Anyone using the inland waterways in France must have an International Certificate of Competence (ICC). To obtain one, you need to be assessed to show that you can handle a vessel to a desired level. The ICC has a time limit, and is only valid for five years, so if you already have one, check the expiry date before you go.

You will also need a CEVNI certificate to show that you have a good working knowledge of the rules and regulations encountered on the inland waterways. To obtain a CEVNI endorsement, you will need to take a test either online or at a training centre.

With the ICC endorsement you should have enough experience to travel along this route. Being able to handle a boat confidently in confined spaces is the most important skill, as between Le Havre and Sète you will encounter over 180 locks. Some of these are manned, others are automatic and operated via remote controls, but you must be able to enter a lock safely, tie up alongside and then leave, while at the same time negotiating a small space with other boats. Some of the locks on the River Rhône are huge, and can be quite daunting to negotiate.

You should travel on the right-hand side of the canal or river, but commercial boats have priority – and as they are often constrained by draught, they will often travel down the centre of the channel. Occasionally they may come round corners on the wrong side, but will usually give a sound signal in warning so you are prepared. If you need to overtake do so on the left-hand side of the vessel, but be aware of any speed limits.

The locks are usually operated by a traffic light system; a single green means it is safe to enter, but make sure you stay well clear of the lock gates until you see this signal as boats may still be manoeuvring out of the lock. Some parts of the canals are also spanned by lifting bridges, not all of which are manned by lock keepers, so you may need to operate them yourself.

Other hazards on the waterways include floating debris, turbulence within the locks, fast-running currents on the Seine and Rhône, and the Mistral, which can cause wind against current and hull windage problems at the southern end of the route.

When to go

France has a temperate climate. Paris and central northern France can experience very variable weather, and plenty of rain, while central to southern France enjoys a more Mediterranean climate, with average summer temperatures reaching 27°C (80°F) and very little, if any, rain. However, during the winter and early spring, southern France can get a battering from the Mistral – a strong and cold northwesterly wind. France's inland waterways can be transited at any time, although May to September or October is best, as the Mediterranean can be very pleasant in the late summer.

left The canals in France offer beauty and tranquillity that is hard to surpass.

THE INLAND WATERWAYS AT A GLANCE

Route length: Approximately 695nm.

Time required: Allow a month if doing a straightforward delivery trip. If you want to explore places en route, allow longer.

When to go: Anytime. Note that work can be done on canals throughout the year, as required.

Weather: France has generally warm summers and mild winters. The closer to the Mediterranean you are, the warmer it gets.

Type and size of boat: Suitable for all types of boats but length is restricted to 98ft (30m) and beam to 5m (15ft). Draught is the biggest constraint, as canal depths vary considerably. A draught of 1.5m is considered the maximum. Yachts must carry their masts unstepped, stowed on deck, or transport them separately by road. Air draught is just 3.5m under most bridges, less if river levels are high.

Equipment: To comply with VNF (French Waterways Authority) rules: mooring lines, reliable engine, lifejackets for each crew member, boat hook, fire extinguishers, bilge pump, navigation lights, horn, search light for tunnels, first-aid kit, courtesy flag, knife, fenders and fenderboard.

Paperwork: Your ICC endorsement, CEVNI certificate, passports for all crew, VNF licence (Vignette) to use the French waterways, vessel's insurance and registration certificates, VHF radio licence and European Waterways Regulations.

Tides: The tidal stretch of the Seine runs from Le Havre to Rouen and tides here can run fast. The Rhône is also well known for its fast-running current, especially near Vallabrègues.

Hazards: Commercial traffic, locks, fast currents, floating debris.

Suitable for night sailing: No private yachts may travel on the tidal section of the Seine at night. Some night-time travel along the inland waterways is possible, although most of the manned locks are only operated 12 hours a day.

Difficulty of route: Medium.

Skills required: Good boat handling skills. Some knowledge of French is also useful.

Charts: *Map of the Inland Waterways of France, Through the French Canals, Carte Des Voies navigables de France* (Editions du Breil).

Berthing/mooring: Alongside berths at town quays. Marinas at Rouen, Paris, Roches-de-Condrieu and Sète.

Ports of entry: Le Havre, Sète.

Water: Readily available from marinas and on town/village quays.

Provisioning: Available in most towns and villages.

Fuel: Available at marinas but carry jerrycans on board so you can fill up at local petrol stations.

Shorepower: Available at marinas and some town and village quays.

Maintenance: Most marinas and ports have boatyards with repair facilities and chandlers, but facilities along some of the canals are minimal.

Family friendliness: Very family friendly.

Further reading: *Inland Waterways of France* by David Edwards-May; *River Seine Cruising Guide* by Derek Bowskill; *Through the French Canals* by David Jefferson; *Floating Through France* by Brenda Davison; *Cruising the Inland Waterways of France & Belgium* by M Harwood, B Davison and R Edgar; *Watersteps Through France* by Bill and Laurel Cooper.

VOYAGE 7

France

THE CÔTE D'AZUR

If you are looking for a cruise with a bit of glitz and glamour, then look no further than the Mediterranean coast of France and the Côte d'Azur. Cannes, Saint-Tropez, Antibes and Monaco have a reputation as the playground of the famous and the rich. The rugged coastline between Marseille and Monaco is home to some of the most luxurious destinations in the world, attracting some of the biggest and most expensive superyachts ever built.

This area has much to offer the more modest boatowner too, with many hidden and relatively inexpensive gems to be discovered along its length. The steep-sided fjord-like inlets known as the Calanques and Îles d'Hyères, 5nm off the mainland port of Hyères, are two destinations worthy of a longer stay. Away from the bright lights of the fashionable resort towns these locations are a welcome dose of reality.

But it's worth visiting the main ports along this coastline, if only for the spectacle they offer. For classic boat enthusiasts visiting during the months of June, September or October there is the incredible sight of some of the most famous yachts in the world, designed by such iconic figures as Fife, Mylne, Sparkman & Stephens and Nicholson, competing on the water during the day before returning to port, their varnishwork gleaming in the warm evening sunlight.

There will probably be a few classic motorboats too – Rivas, Chris-Craft and Fairey runabouts – and if you ignore the bright white gin palaces that berth fender to fender in the marinas, it's like stepping back in time to a bygone age.

below The route ends in Monaco, which is famous for its connections with the rich and famous.

The route

This route extends for 130nm from Marseille, midway along the French Mediterranean coast, to the sovereign city-state of Monaco. Calling in en route at some of the off-lying islands, it offers a mix of marina and anchorage destinations and a variety of choices to suit most budgets. At peak season parts of this cruise can be very expensive, particularly if you stop at some of the bigger marinas, so it is wise to plan your cruise in detail before departure. Many of the busier marinas operate on a reservation basis only and others will only allow a single night's stay for visitors.

The starting point is the city of Marseille, from where it is a short sail to the Calanques, the series of inlets and bays that dominate the coastline. From here it is another short hop to La Ciotat and its Vieux Port, which offers good facilities, restaurants and shopping at reasonable prices. Another 30nm sail will bring you to the Îles d'Hyères, an archipelago made up of four islands. The biggest one, Île de Porquerolles, is the main attraction. Although its marina is often jam-packed, there are several anchorages to choose from which offer good access ashore.

From here, head to Île de Port-Cros and Île du Levant before continuing northeast to the glitz and glamour of Saint-Tropez, calling in at the delightful anchorage of Cap Taillat en route. From Saint-Tropez, it is another 25nm hop to Cannes and then a further 7nm to Antibes. Villefranche and St-Jean-Cap-Ferrat on the eastern side of Nice are worth a visit, before completing the final 8nm to the last destination at Monaco.

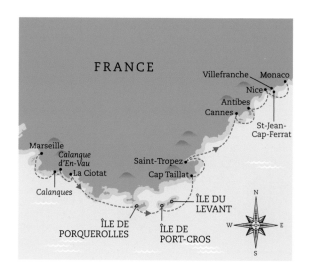

left La Ciotat has plenty of restaurants and facilities and can be a less expensive option than some of the other ports.

Destinations

Marseille: The second-largest city in France is the first destination on this cruise. Marking the gateway to the Côte d'Azur, the city was once the region's most important centre for trade and today is still the country's biggest commercial port. For visiting yachts it has much to offer, particularly at its Vieux Port. Sites to visit include the lighthouse Phare de Saint Marie built in 1855, the 3rd-century Abbaye St Victor and the Musée des Civilisations de l'Europe et de la Méditerranée. Shopping and facilities for yachts are excellent.

Calanques: Away from the hubbub of city life, the Calanques are definitely worth a visit. These inlets and bays pepper the coastline for 11nm between Marseille and Cassis and provide a number of anchorages in stunning settings. Of them all, Calanque d'En-Vau near Cassis is probably the most stunning, with near-vertical white limestone cliffs fringing a bay of turquoise water. In peak season anchoring room is limited, but visit early in the season and you'll have plenty of space to yourself.

La Ciotat: This working town is where the superyachts now come to be repaired or fitted out, but it has much to offer the cruising sailor too. It isn't that expensive in comparison with other ports along this coast. The beach, although artificial, is good, as is the shopping, and the facilities at the Port Vieux are worth a visit.

Îles d'Hyères: This group of four islands is one of the gems of this area. Less popular than the main resorts of this coastline, the islands offer a number of anchorages as well as a marina and facilities on the largest of the islands, Île de Porquerolles. The beaches here are very good, as are the walks ashore, and the heavily forested Île de Port-Cros is home to a national park.

Saint-Tropez: This town is one of the places that you should not miss if cruising the Côte d'Azur. While expensive, the old harbour and the town that flanks it are delightful, and in some parts quite traditional too. It gets packed in peak season, and in late September/early October during Les Voiles de Saint-Tropez, the major regatta, but there are places nearby that offer more access at less expense. Port Grimaud to the west is massive but facilities are excellent, while Sainte-Maxime to the north is usually better value. The only real anchorage is in the Baie de Canebiers, immediately to the east of Saint-Tropez – but don't try anchoring in the Golfe de Saint-Tropez as the bay is very deep indeed.

Cannes: You are spoilt for choice at Cannes with three marinas within the glitzy town. Expect it to be busy year-round – there is plenty to see and do, including visiting the Musée d'Art d'Histoire de Provence and the town's numerous festivals and events. Quieter anchorages can be found off the Îles de Lérins, a group of four islands immediately to the south of the town. Of these Île Sainte-Marguerite is perhaps the best known for its inhabitant, the Man in the Iron Mask, a prisoner who moved to the island in 1687.

Villefranche: This town, immediately adjacent to the city of Nice, is a delightful place to stay. It is well sheltered and cheaper than Nice but the facilities are just as good. An anchorage on the east coast of St-Jean-Cap-Ferrat offers good protection too.

Monaco: The final port of call is probably the least attractive, as it really is the most expensive on this route. The main harbour, Port de Hercules, is right in the thick of it, but it is generally packed with superyachts. Port Fontvieille-Monaco does not usually have visitors' berths available for boats.

Level of skill

You don't need any particular skills, or level of skills, to navigate the waters of the Côte d'Azur. Eyeball navigation is all that is required, as tides and tidal currents are minimal in this part of the Mediterranean.

The biggest hazard you will come up against during this cruise is other boats. Peak season is July and August, when these waters can get very busy. This can make negotiating your way in or out of a marina or harbour a tricky operation. Not all boat users in this area have a high level of skills, and such is the size of some of the boats that occupy these marina berths that they require plenty of room in which to manoeuvre. Keep a good lookout at all times when entering or leaving marinas or ports, and if necessary stay well clear.

One of the side effects of so many boats in close proximity is the wash that can be produced – and consequently swell and rough water. Unfortunately this can have an adverse effect on some of the otherwise attractive anchorages along this coast, making some of them untenable in all but the most settled conditions.

One skill that is important is the ability to berth stern- or bow-to the dock. Space within most of the marinas along this route is at a premium, so being able to berth quickly and efficiently is a must. Similarly,

anchorages in the Calanques can get quite crowded in peak season and most have minimal swinging room. The best option is therefore to anchor relatively close inshore and then take a long line ashore and attach it to a rock or tree to avoid any difficulty in berthing.

When to go

Mediterranean France enjoys a long summer season, and consequently you can cruise this route any time between late April and October. The summer months can get very busy, particularly so in August when most of Europe shuts down for its summer holidays. If possible avoid peak season and aim for either early or late in the year, when unoccupied marina berths are more prevalent and prices tend to be lower.

Temperatures in this region average 25–30°C (77–86°F) during July and August, while the winter months are usually mild, with the wettest months being in late autumn. Winds in this area tend to be fairly light, with brisker winds blowing up off the shore in the afternoon. In early spring the region can be affected by the strong cold northwesterly wind of the Mistral. Gales can batter this coastline during the winter months, and as late as April or as early as October, so check the forecasts before setting sail.

THE CÔTE D'AZUR AT A GLANCE

Route length: Around 130nm.

Time required: Two to three weeks.

When to go: Late April to October.

Weather: Mediterranean climate: dry, hot summers, wet and mild winters. Temperatures average 29°C (84°F) in August.

Type and size of boat: Power or sail, 25ft (7.6m) plus.

Equipment: Charts, chartplotter, depth sounder, reliable engine.

Tides: Minimal tidal range and currents.

Hazards: Other boats. This coastline, particularly around the main destinations such as Saint-Tropez, Cannes, Antibes and Monaco, can get very busy with other boats during peak season so keep a good lookout. Wash from powerboats can be a problem too.

Suitable for night sailing: Yes, most of the harbours and marinas are well lit and the approach is straightforward. This area can get busy with leisure craft, however, so keep a good lookout at all times.

Difficulty of route: Easy.

Skills required: Ability to keep a good lookout and berth stern- and bow-to, as well as good practical experience of anchoring in close quarters.

Charts: Imray: M15 (Marseille to San Remo), M40 (Ligurian and Tyrrhenian Seas), M16 (Ligurian Sea). Admiralty: 2116 (France – South coast; Foz-sur-Mer to Marseilles), 153 (Approaches to Marseille), 1705 (Cabo de San Sebastian to Îles d'Hyères), 2120 (France – South Coast; Toulon to Cavalaire-sur-Mer including Îles d'Hyères), 2166 (Cap Camarat to Cannes), 1974 (Toulon to San Remo including Northern Corse), 1998 (Nice to Livorno including Gulf of Genoa), 351 (Ports in the Gulf of Genoa).

Berthing/mooring: Most of the major towns along this route have marina berths available, offering bow- or stern-to berthing.

Ports of entry: Marseilles, Hyères, Antibes, Nice, Cannes, Saint-Tropez, Monaco.

Water: Available at most marinas along the route.

Provisioning: Widely available at towns along the route.

Fuel: Available at most marinas along the route.

Shorepower: Available at most marinas along the route.

Maintenance: Range of services available at marinas along the route.

Family friendliness: This route is very family friendly with lots of beaches, places to explore and things to do ashore.

Further reading: *Mediterranean France & Corsica Pilot* by Rod and Lucinda Heikell.

left The four islands that make up the Îles d'Hyères are one of the highlights of this cruise, with stunning anchorages.

VOYAGE 8

Spain

THE NORTHWEST COAST

Fringing the southwestern shores of the Bay of Biscay, the Galicia coast is a real gem of a destination. Stunning beaches, deep, fjord-like inlets and charming towns and villages steeped in history make this area a fascinating place to explore, and one that is relatively quiet and unspoiled in comparison to many Spanish ports.

Most visiting yachts tend to be on passage either north or south, with the excellent facilities at La Coruña providing a good stopover for boats bound to or from the Bay of Biscay. However, this area deserves exploration time in its own right, and with plenty to see or do, a cruise along the Galician coast from Ribadeo to Camariñas can be very rewarding.

The biggest attraction of this stretch of mainland Spain is its rías – a series of long, narrow, tidal inlets or 'drowned river valleys' that punctuate the coastline. Of the many rías found in Spain, and indeed Portugal too, it is those that form the Rías Altas, or 'Upper Rias', that provide the most interest.

The Rías Bajas, or 'Lower Rias', farther to the south, while spectacular in places, are far more touristy as holiday destinations, so the Rías Altas are more appealing if you are looking for a remote place to explore.

Despite some potential hazards the route offers good sailing conditions and facilities, and the majority of the harbours are still very traditional. Ashore there is plenty to see too, both historical and cultural, and sites such as the city of Santiago de Compostela and the Tower of Hercules at La Coruña are within easy reach.

below La Coruña has plenty of facilities and a wealth of historical connections.

The route

This route covers around 104nm of Galicia on the northwest coast of Spain. Starting at Ribadeo on the Ría de Ribadeo, 139nm west of Bilbao, it concludes at Camariñas, which lies 16nm to the north of Cape Finisterre. Although the route is linear, it offers numerous places to visit along the way, and can either serve as a stopover point as part of a longer cruise or as a destination in its own right.

The first port of call after leaving Ribadeo is the Ría de Vivero, the first of the main Rías Altas. From there the next ría, the Ría del Barquero, can be explored, before heading west around the Iberian Peninsula's northernmost point – Punta de la Estaca de Bares – towards the Ría de Santa Marta de Ortigueira. This ría should not be missed as parts of it are stunning. From there, continue to the Ría de Cedeira, a popular destination but one that can be entered in any conditions, and then on to La Coruña – Galicia's capital and a fascinating place to visit. Camariñas, approximately 35nm to the southwest, is the final port of call on this route, and a favourite to many – its large, sheltered bay providing an attractive location to conclude your cruise.

left Ría de Cedeira can get busy in high season but its steep wooded hills make it a lovely destination.

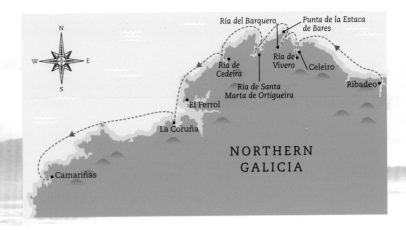

Destinations

Ría de Ribadeo: The first ría on this route is accessible in all but northerly gales, with a wide, open entrance that is easily identified by its twin lighthouses and the road bridge that spans it immediately to the north of the town of Ribadeo. Here you'll find two marinas – the Darsena de Porcillan Marina and another operated by the Club Nautico de Ribadeo – and a delightful town that sits high above the harbour. Shallow-draught boats can also explore the southern half of the ría, where some pretty anchorages can be found, although sandbanks do feature.

Ría de Vivero: You'll find another large ría, the Ría de Vivero, 30nm farther west. Again, accessible in all but northerly winds, it offers several fair-weather anchorages, as well as berths at Celeiro and Vivero. The historic town of Vivero is well worth a visit as parts of the town date to the 12th century, and its annual festivals are some of the oldest in Galicia.

Ría del Barquero: The last ría on this stretch of north coast, before you reach the Punta de la Estaca de Bares – Spain's northernmost headland – is the Ría del Barquero. This wide, open ría is fringed by beaches, several of which can be anchored off as can the village of Puerto de Bares. Facilities here are minimal, but the location is stunning.

Ría de Santa Marta de Ortigueira: Despite the wide bay that marks the entrance, few boats venture farther than the Isla San Vicente owing to the sandbar and sandbanks here. One of the prettiest rías in this area, it winds gently inland through densely wooded hills to the town of Santa Marta de Ortigueira, where there is a small town quay. You can anchor nearby too, but beware of the shifting sands.

Ría de Cedeira: Accessible in most conditions, the Ría de Cedeira lies southwest of Punta de la Estaca de Bares. Steep-sided hills fringe the deep inlet and the beaches at Playa de Cedeira and Playa de Loira are some of the best on this coastline. It is a stunning place to visit, although often busy with boats on passage to or from the Bay of Biscay, and during August hordes of tourists descend.

La Coruña: This is the largest destination on the route, and one of the most popular too. It is well supplied with facilities and services catering for visiting sailors, and the town includes several sights of interest. Of these the Torre de Hercules, a lighthouse that was built by the Romans in the 1st century AD and is still in operation, is one of the most interesting, although the harbour also has a famous connection as the place the Spanish Armada left from in 1588.

Camariñas: The final port of call, which lies to the south of Cabo Villano, is an attractive ría that is a popular destination for visiting yachts. Beware Las Quebrantas, an unmarked reef to the northwest of the entrance, and the regular movement of fishing boats that are based here. Facilities at Camariñas are good, as is the food, and there are also several anchorages in the northeast corner of the ría.

right Ría de Vivero, home to a 12th-century town, offers plenty of good anchorages.

Level of skill

Lying so close to the Bay of Biscay and the main shipping route to and from Northern Europe, the northwest coast has its own challenges. However, the beauty of this area is that its rías offer excellent shelter, and although not all are suitable in all wind directions, if one isn't, another will be. Most of the rías are just an easy daysail away, so if the weather deteriorates, shelter should be within close reach.

It pays, however, to plan your route carefully, with contingencies for poor weather conditions. Although high skill levels are not required to cruise this area, this is nevertheless a coastline with a notorious reputation. Exposed to the worst of the North Atlantic gales in the autumn and winter months, this is a coast that is best visited in the summer months when it can be idyllic, with not even a hint of the coastline's potential malevolence being evident.

However, be aware that fog, particularly in the summer months, can be a very real hazard. It is not unusual for it to be so thick that you can't see beyond the cockpit, and it will often linger well into the afternoon. Heavy swell can also be a problem following bad weather, particularly on the Atlantic coast, which can make entering harbours tricky, so again it is important to plan properly.

Galicia is heavily dominated by its fishing industry, with most of the ports and harbours that you will visit catering primarily for working boats. A good lookout is therefore essential, particularly if fog rolls in.

In many of the rías themselves you will also encounter mussel rafts, few of which are lit, so if travelling around at night stick to the main channels. The closer you get to Cape Finisterre, which lies to the south of Camariñas, the more shipping you are likely to encounter too. A Traffic Separation Scheme (TSS) is in operation approximately 20nm west of Cape Finisterre, and although of little relevance to boats cruising this coastline, a good lookout should be maintained in the vicinity, particularly as some of the larger offshore fishing trawlers are based along this stretch of coast.

When to go

Dominated by the North Atlantic weather patterns, the northwest coast of Spain enjoys a very different climate from the southern part of the country. Temperatures in Galicia average 19–20°C (66–68°F) in July, whereas on the Mediterranean coast temperatures are often in excess of 30°C (86°F). The winter months are usually mild, but rain is a regular occurrence throughout the year – even in June and July – and the western part of the route often gets a battering from Atlantic storms.

The prevailing winds in this area are generally northwesterly or southwesterly, although during the summer months more northerly winds can be experienced. Expect localized anomalies too on the north coast of Galicia and within the rías themselves, and occasional ferocious squalls.

The biggest consideration when planning to sail this route is when to arrive at Ribadeo. From mid-August onwards, the Bay of Biscay can be a treacherous place if heavy weather rolls in, so it is best to plan your Galician cruise around when a crossing of the Bay needs to be made. Generally, however, the best time to explore these waters is between May and August.

THE NORTHWEST COAST AT A GLANCE

Route length: Approximately 104nm.

Time required: Three weeks.

When to go: May to August. If arriving via the Bay of Biscay, avoid crossing from late August onwards as weather conditions can deteriorate significantly then.

Weather: Temperatures in July and August average 19–20°C (66–68°F), while winters are usually mild, although very wet. Northwesterly and southwesterly winds prevail, but parts of the north coast can have its own weather patterns, including ferocious squalls.

Type and size of boat: No particular restrictions on size or type, although a cruising boat of 25–45ft (7.6–13.7m) is about right.

Equipment: Chartplotter, depth sounder, radar reflector and/or responder, decent anchor, AIS.

Tides: At Springs, tidal range is around 3m, while at Neaps it is around 1.5m. Tidal streams are usually minimal – around ½ knot.

Hazards: Heavy shipping, fishing boats, fog, rocks and shoals, heavy swell, mussel rafts.

Suitable for night sailing: Yes, most harbours between Ribadeo and Camariñas are well lit, but watch out for unlit mussel rafts and sandbanks in the rías, as well as rocks near the entrances.

Difficulty of route: Moderate.

Skills required: Basic navigation and pilotage skills, as well as an ability to anchor. Excellent lookout skills too, due to the number of fishing boats in this area and the regular occurrence of fog.

Charts: Admiralty: 1113 (Harbours on the NorthWest Coast of Spain), 1122 (Ports on the North Coast of Spain). Imray: C48 (La Coruña to Porto), C45 (Santander to La Coruña).

Berthing/mooring: Most rías offer both alongside marina or town quay berths and places to anchor.

Ports of entry: La Coruña, El Ferrol.

Water: Available at most towns within the rías.

Provisioning: Food and drink is widely available, and spares can be found in the bigger ports, such as La Coruña, La Camariñas and Ribadeo.

Fuel: Available at the marinas at La Coruña, La Camariñas and Ribadeo.

Shorepower: Available at the marinas at La Coruña, La Camariñas and Ribadeo.

Maintenance: La Coruña offers the best yacht repair and engineer services on this route, although some of the marinas in the smaller towns may be able to provide limited help.

Family friendliness: Spain is a wonderful place to visit with children, and with plenty of beaches and places to explore on this route, there is plenty to entertain them.

Further reading: *South Biscay Pilot* by RCCPF/Steve Pickard; *Cruising Galicia* by Carlos Rojas and Robert Bailey; *Atlantic Spain & Portugal* by RCCPF, Martin Walker and Henry Bu.

VOYAGE 9
Italy

SICILY AND ITS ISLANDS

Measuring 25,711sq km (9,927 square miles), Sicily is the largest island in the Mediterranean, and one of the most attractive too. It lies just 1.6nm off the southern tip of Italy, separated by the Strait of Messina, and bordered by the Mediterranean, Tyrrhenian and Ionian seas.

The island is one of dramatic contrasts: crystal-clear cobalt waters, delightful sandy beaches and historic towns fringe much of its coastline, while its interior is a mix of towering mountain ranges that dominate the north coast, lower-lying hills to the south and the imposing spectacle of the 3,329m (10,922ft)-high Mount Etna, Europe's largest active volcano, which to this day continues to smoulder gently on Sicily's east coast.

Volcanoes also dominate much of the Aeolian Islands, an archipelago of eight islands that stands 16nm off the northeast coast of Sicily, and is a gem of a destination for cruising yachtsmen. The Egadi Islands off the western tip of Sicily, which are home to the largest tuna fishing industry in this part of the Mediterranean, provide interest too, and can be a very pleasant place to spend a day or two.

Historically, Sicily and its satellite islands have had a very chequered past. Like the Ionian Islands to the south (see p68), the history of Sicily is marked by its many rulers. Nearly every ancient civilization in the Mediterranean – including the Romans, Greeks, Normans, Arabs, Byzantines and Ostrogoths – have at one time ruled the island, and consequently it is rich in archeological and architectural sites of interest, with a real mish-mash of styles. It's a fascinating place to explore, and by sea is the perfect way.

below The Egadi Islands, which lie to the west of Sicily, offer stunning harbours and dramatic landscapes.

The route

This is a circular cruise, which starts and ends in the delightful city of Syracuse on Sicily's southeast coast. Sailing clockwise around Sicily, the first part of the cruise, along the island's south and west coasts, is only of particular interest if you are looking for a beach to anchor off. However, once you have reached the three Egadi (or Aegadian) Islands, which lie 7nm off Trapani on the western tip of Sicily, the real cruise begins.

The small mountainous islands – Favignana, Levanzo and Marettimo – which are home to around just 5,000 people, offer several anchorages set amid dramatic scenery.

From here, Sicily's north coast can then be explored. The northwestern corner is highly appealing, with its spectacular cliffs, rock stacks and small beach-fringed bays, but to the east lie charming harbours at Palermo and Cefalu.

The Aeolian Islands, which lie 16nm off Sicily's north coast, should also be explored. This archipelago of eight volcanic islands is simply stunning and worth making the time for. From the Aeolian Islands the route continues via the eastern corner of Sicily and the Strait of Messina to Taormina on the east coast, a town that is a lovely place to visit. Catania, around 35nm to the south, is also worth visiting, before completing the route and a circumnavigation of Sicily at Syracuse.

below Cefalu is a good place to anchor, offering a large bay, beach and medieval streets.

Destinations

Syracuse: This ancient metropolis dates from 734 BCE and was once thought to be the ancient world's most beautiful city. Today, it is recognized as a UNESCO World Heritage Site, and is a fascinating place to explore. Sites to visit include the 5th century BCE Greek theatre to the northwest of Syracuse and the 7th century Temple of Apollo, which stands on Ortygia, an offshore island accessed via a bridge. Berths are available for visitors in the marina or alongside the town quay, and there is room to anchor in the harbour.

Egadi Islands: Comprising three islands – Favignana, Levanzo and Marettimo – the Egadi Islands are a protected marine reserve and lie about 7nm offshore of Trapani. Well known for their tuna fishery – the largest in Sicily – and the Mattanza festival on Favignana, the islands also offer several anchorages. Expect them to be popular with daytrippers during the peak season.

Palermo: The city of Palermo is Sicily's capital and consequently very popular with tourists. Handy for its travel links, including its proximity to an airport, you will be spoilt for things to see in the city, historical and cultural. Visiting boats can berth in the harbour or at Marina Villa Igiea, immediately to the north of the city.

Cefalu: Heading 39nm east from Palermo, along the north coast of Sicily, the next town of interest is Cefalu. This medieval town flanks a large bay, which can offer somewhere to anchor in settled conditions. Ashore, you'll find a good beach, winding narrow streets and a beautiful cathedral that dates to 1131.

Aeolian Islands: The real gem of this cruise lies 16nm off the north coast of Sicily. The volcanic Aeolian Islands are a stunning destination, offering idyllic anchorages in cobalt seas, while ashore there is much to see and do among the rugged landscape. Avoid them during peak season, however, as the eight islands in the archipelago can become saturated with visitors, and anchorages extremely crowded. Out of season this can be an idyllic place to explore, with Lipari, Salina and Panarea being of most interest.

Taormina: During the summer months the ancient Greek amphitheatre at Taormina is the setting for numerous rock and classical music events, as well as a film festival and ballet performances. An interesting place to visit, the town lies at the southern end of the Strait of Messina and is a popular destination with tourists. Limited mooring buoys are available here, but a reasonable anchorage can be found 15nm to the south at Naxos.

Catania: Another Roman amphitheatre can be found at Catania, midway down Sicily's east coast, but the most dramatic landmark here, at whose feet Catania lies, is Mount Etna. The volcano has had a significant impact on the town, having destroyed it on several occasions, and the town offers some stunning views of the smouldering UNESCO World Heritage Site.

Level of skill

You don't require a lot of experience to cruise in this area, although good experience of anchoring, particularly in crowded waters, is essential. The north coast and Aeolian Islands can get very busy peak season, so be prepared to manoeuvre and anchor in close vicinity to other boats, well away from isolated rocks. Keep an eye on the weather, as some of the anchorages can be untenable and exposed if swell or strong winds roll in.

The biggest hazard on this cruise is the Strait of Messina, which separates mainland Italy and Sicily, in the island's northeastern corner. At its narrowest point, between Punta del Faro on Sicily and the town of Villa San Giovanni in Calabria in southern Italy, it measures just 1.6nm, and the waters in this area can be relatively congested with boats. A Traffic Separation Scheme (TSS) operates in this area, which includes a 'roundabout-type system' to the west of Villa San Giovanni to allow for boats moving between mainland Italy and Sicily. Most pleasure boat users do not need to enter the TSS, but if you do, then you must contact Messina VTS on VHF Channels 10 or 14.

You will find that the Strait of Messina is very popular with local fishermen, especially in May and August when swordfish are sought. To catch the swordfish, fishermen use unusual looking boats, controlled by the helmsman and his spotters, who stand at the top of a 30m (98ft)-high mast. A harpoonist stands at the end of a 45m (148ft)-long 'feluche' or walkway to creep up on swordfish undetected. If you see these boats operating nearby, give them a wide berth.

As the narrow Strait of Messina is the point where the Tyrrhenian Sea meets the Ionian Sea, the seabed changes in height and tidal currents here can be tricky. Avoid the Strait in wind-over-tide conditions, and watch out for unusual counter-currents close inshore. Whirlpools occur here frequently too.

When to go

Sicily and the Aeolian Islands benefit from a Mediterranean climate, and so are best explored from mid-April to October. Temperatures in May and June average 22–25°C (72–77°F), so this is a good time to visit at the start of the season. In July and August temperatures average 29°C (84°F) and the area can be overrun with tourists and visiting yachts. In September and October, at the end of the season, the temperatures average 22–26°C (72–79°F).

The summer months are generally dry, with most rainfall occurring during the winter. The prevailing northwesterlies tend to be light, but this area can be affected by the sirocco during the spring and autumn. The sirocco, which can often be storm force, originates in North Africa. The sand carried over by the sirocco from the Sahara can reduce visibility offshore.

SICILY AND ITS ISLANDS AT A GLANCE

Route length: A circumnavigation of Sicily is around 653nm, but the route is longer if you visit the Aeolian Islands, 16nm off Sicily's north coast.

Time required: Three to four weeks.

When to go: Mid-April to October. Avoid peak season, as parts of Sicily, and particularly the Aeolian Islands, can get very overcrowded.

Weather: Dry, hot summers and wet, mild winters. Temperatures peak season average 29°C (84°F).

Type and size of boat: Average-sized cruising boats are ideal: 25–45ft (7.6–13.7m). Anchorages can be crowded and moorings expensive in peak season, so smaller boats may be preferable then.

Equipment: Chartplotter, depth sounder, decent anchor.

Tides: Tidal range is minimal, but tidal streams within the Strait of Messina can be strong at times.

Hazards: Off-lying rocks and reefs, fishing boats, ferries and daytripper boats, tidal currents and TSS within the Strait of Messina.

Suitable for night sailing: Yes, although the chart should be studied carefully for off-lying rocks. Avoid the Strait of Messina, which can be busy with commercial boats.

Difficulty of route: Easy to moderate.

Skills required: A good, practical knowledge of anchoring and pilotage skills.

Charts: Admiralty: 1440 (Adriatic Sea), 2123 (Capo Granitola to Capo Passero), 1941 (Capo Passero to Capo Colonne), 172 (Isole Eolie), 805 (Ports in the Tyrrhenian Sea), 1018 (Approaches to Stretto di Messina), 1976 (Capo di Bonifati to Capo San Vito), 963 (Ports on the North Coast of Sicilia), 965 (Ports on the South Coast of Sicilia), 964 (Sicilia West Coast). Imray: M31 (Sicily), M47 (Aeolian Islands), M19 (Capo Palinuro to Punta Stilo), M30 (Southern Adriatic and Ionian Seas).

Berthing/mooring: Numerous marinas around Sicily, including at Trapani, Palermo, Portorosa, Riposto, Catania, Syracuse and Licata. Some towns, such as Taormina, have mooring buoys offshore for visitor use, and there are many anchorages, although not all are suitable in all conditions.

Ports of entry: Marsala, Trapani, Palermo, Messina, Porto Empedocle, Catania, Syracuse, Gela.

Water: Available at most marinas.

Provisioning: Available at most of the towns and cities along the route. Be aware that prices in the Aeolian Islands are often notoriously high.

Fuel: Available at most marinas.

Shorepower: Available at the larger marinas.

Maintenance: Most of the marinas at the larger destinations, such as Syracuse and Palermo, can offer boat maintenance and servicing.

Family friendliness: Good. Plenty of beaches and places to explore. Most of the destinations are just a short daysail away.

Further reading: *Italian Waters Pilot* by Rod Heikell.

left Taormina is the site of an ancient Greek amphitheatre and well worth a visit.

VOYAGE 10

Croatia

THE DALMATIAN COAST

For a long time, Croatia's Dalmatian coast has been one of the hidden gems of the Adriatic. Undiscovered by hordes of tourists and charter boats until relatively recently, the 170nm stretch of coastline between Zadar and Dubrovnik and its myriad off-lying islands has been the cruising destination of comparatively few. Today, however, the secret is more widely known and the area now rivals Greece as one of the most popular destinations in the Mediterranean.

Croatia's charm is due, in part, to its combination of dramatic coastal scenery and rugged islands, mixed with the historic beauty of the numerous medieval harbours that pepper the mainland. Despite the fact that many of these ports saw significant damage during the Croatian War of Independence (1991–95), the majority of these historic towns have since been sympathetically restored. Their sympathetic restoration, however, means these towns and harbours have been able to regain much of their original character. Combine this with good facilities, shopping and nightlife, and the stunning natural beauty of places such as the Kornati Islands and Krka National Park, and you have a destination that would sit high on anyone's list.

The sailing is pretty good too. Minimal tides, warm dry summers and decent sea breezes make this destination suitable for novice and experienced sailors alike, and if you want to avoid marinas during the peak season, then there's a diverse range of anchorages to choose from, many of which are often deserted. It's a place with something for everyone that has to be explored.

below The city of Dubrovnik, where this cruise starts, is a World Heritage Site and one of the finest cities in Europe.

The route

This route is a linear cruise that travels up the Dalmatian coast from Dubrovnik northwest to the Kornati Islands. The starting destination is the superb city of Dubrovnik, at the southern end of the Dalmatian coast. From here, head northwest to the island of Mljet and the small settlement at Polače on the island's northern coast, a distance of about 35nm.

Then, continue north-northwest for 22nm until you reach the next destination of Korčula Island and the town of Korčula on its northeastern coast. Heading west via the Peljeski Kanal and the south coast of the Peljesac peninsula, the next destination is the island of Vis, 49nm away. Here you will find Kormiža on the west coast, before heading clockwise round the island to Vis Town, which fringes a large bay on the north coast.

The route then continues on a northeasterly heading to the Pakleni Islands, which lie off the southwestern coast of Hvar Island, another interesting place to explore, 22nm north-east of Kormiža. Of the numerous islets, Sveti Klement, the largest in the group, is the most attractive and there is a marina on the northeastern tip of the island.

From Sveti Klement head north via the channel between the islands of Šolta and Brač to the mainland port of Split. The cruise then follows the coast west and then north to Šibenik, from where Skradin and the Krka National Park up the River Krka can be explored. Or, head east towards the Kornati Islands, the final destination.

below Sparkling seas and rocky inlets are a major feature of this cruise.

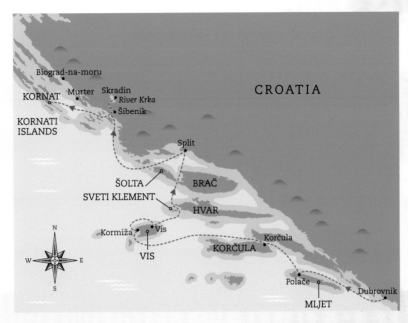

Destinations

Dubrovnik: Formerly named Ragusa, this World Heritage Site is one of the finest cities in Europe. Medieval in origin, during the 16th and 17th centuries it was a key harbour within the Adriatic, and home to around 200 ships. Large parts of the city were destroyed during the Croatian War of Independence, when the walled city was under siege for nine months, but today much of it has been restored. Sites to see include the magnificent city walls that encircle the Old Town, the 14th-century Franciscan monastery and museum, and Luza Square in the centre of the town. Facilities for boat owners are excellent, with a 425-berth marina at the head of the Rijeka Dubrovačka river.

Mljet: This lush, green island lies 35nm northwest of Dubrovnik, and while the south coast of the island is exposed and offers few places to anchor, the Mljet National Park at the western end of the island gives you several alternatives. Facilities other than restaurants and basic provisions are minimal on the island, but the island's lakes and forests are well worth exploring.

Korčula: Lying immediately to the south of the Pelješac peninsula, Korčula is a long, thin island with a fascinating history. Its main settlement, Korčula Town, which sits on the northeastern coast, is a charming fortified medieval town and the likely birthplace of Marco Polo. Along with the historic locations, the shops and market are worth visiting too.

Hvar: Directly north of Korčula is Hvar, another long, thin island that is a popular destination with cruising boats. Jagged inlets and fields of lavender dominate this island, which is also home to several vineyards on its southern shores. Hvar Town itself is usually busy with tripper boats, and in recent years has seen much commercialization. The Pakleni Islands immediately to the south of the town offer alternative places to stay overnight.

Krka National Park: If you wind your way inland up the River Krka from Šibenik, you will find yourself at Skradin, a small village and marina. Boat trips from here will then take you to the Krka National Park, through which the River Krka flows. The 17 waterfalls that fall in this area are stunning, and it is a beautiful diversion away from the island destinations.

Kornati Islands: This archipelago of 152 islands and islets is scattered around the main island of Kornat, which lies to the southwest of Biograd-na-moru on the Croatian mainland. Now looked after by the Kornati National Park, these islands were once owned by Zadar's nobility and managed by local sheep farmers, who also grew olive trees here. The islands are packed with places to explore, but before visiting you should check where you can anchor overnight as some restrictions do apply to protect the islands' natural habitat. Careful study of the chart is also recommended for safe passage through the islands.

Level of skill

One of the many attractions of this cruising destination is that you don't need to be an expert sailor to enjoy it. With care, this is an area that can be explored by all, and even novice sailors will find themselves able to navigate its waters. Tides here are minimal and with plenty of destinations within easy reach of each other, it's not hard to find places to overnight or stop for lunch, or even run for shelter if conditions deteriorate.

The biggest hazard along this stretch of coast is the numerous islands, islets and shoals that litter it. In some places, such as the Kornati Archipelago, islands and islets number over 150 in a relatively small sea area, so a good lookout and careful studying of the chart is essential. Most of the area is well buoyed, so it is possible to follow the channels between the islands and approaches to the harbours easily. However, sailing within this area at night is not recommended, as although many channels are lit, the sheer number of unmarked rocks and shoals make it quite hazardous. Even sailing here in poor visibility is not recommended.

Winds along this stretch of coast are predominately from the northwest, and although the bora – a katabatic wind that affects the Adriatic – is a threat, this is only really a problem during the winter months. Thunderstorms are, however, a regular occurrence during the summer, and often appear out of nowhere,

above The ancient town of Korčula is thought to be the birthplace of Marco Polo.

along with violent gusts. Maestrals – anabatic sea breezes that blow all day before easing at night – are also common during the summer months .

A good knowledge of anchoring is useful as there are a number of delightful anchorages along this route. It is useful to have some experience of bow- and stern-to berthing as well. Most of the marinas and quays at harbours along this coast and on the islands only offer this type of berthing. Lazylines are often used, however, which does make berthing easier.

When to go

Croatia enjoys a typical Mediterranean climate, with mild winters and hot, dry summers. The sailing season runs from April to October and, like Greece, outside these times many of the shoreside cafés and restaurants close down. Temperatures in peak season, during July and August, regularly reach in excess of 30°C (86°F) and while the sea breeze helps to cool things down, on the mainland coast it can get very hot and crowded. Although the islands offer myriad opportunities to anchor, visiting at either end of the season in April/May or September/October is often preferable.

THE DALMATION COAST AT A GLANCE

Route length: Around 200nm.

Time required: Two to three weeks would give you a good overview of the area, but allow longer if you want to explore further, as the Kornati Islands in particular are of great appeal.

When to go: April to October.

Weather: Typical Mediterranean climate – hot, dry summers, mild winters. Average summer temperatures are 25–30°C (77–86°F), but they regularly exceed this during July and August. Decent sea breezes keep things cool.

Type and size of boat: Power or sail, 25ft (7.6m) plus.

Equipment: Charts, binoculars, chartplotter, depth sounder, anchor, bimini.

Tides: Minimal tidal range. Tidal currents around 0.5 knots, although stronger in narrow channels.

Hazards: Rocks and shoals, thunderstorms and associated squalls, unexploded landmines left over from the Croatian War of Independence on the hills ashore, so stick to the main paths!

Suitable for night sailing: Not recommended.

Difficulty of route: Easy to moderate.

Skills required: Ability to berth stern- or bow-to with lazylines and a good, practical knowledge of anchoring, as well as basic pilotage and navigation skills.

Charts: Imray: M25 (Otok Rab to Sibenik), M26 (Split to Dubrovnik), M23 (Adriatic Sea Passage Chart), M27 Dubrovnik to Bar and Ulcinj. Admiralty: 2711 (Rogoznica to Zadar), 2774 (Otok Vis to Sibenik), 2712 (Otok Susac to Split), 1574 (Otok Glavat to Ploce and Makarska), 1580 (Otocic Veliki Skolk to Otocic Glavat), 680 (Dubrovnik), 269 (Ploce and Split with adjacent harbours, channels and anchorages).

Berthing/mooring: Numerous marinas along the coast and on the larger islands. Mooring buoys in protected areas, such as national parks, where anchoring is not allowed. However, there is a huge choice of places to anchor off many of the islands, which are suitable in a variety of conditions.

Ports of entry: Hvar, Split, Korčula, Murter, Dubrovnik.

Water: Widely available at marinas along the route and at most harbours.

Provisioning: Available at all ports along the coast and at many of the island destinations.

Fuel: Widely available at marinas along the route.

Shorepower: Widely available at marinas along the route.

Maintenance: Most of the larger marinas, such as at Dubrovnik, Split and Skradin, have facilities and boatyard services that will meet most needs, including slipways, cranes and travel hoists.

Family friendliness: Very family friendly. Plenty of activities for children. Short distances between the islands mean passages don't need to be long.

Further reading: *The Croatia Cruising Companion* by Jane Cody and John Nash; *Adriatic Pilot* by Trevor and Dinah Thompson; *777 Harbours & Anchorages* by Karl H Bestanding.

VOYAGE 11

Greece

THE IONIAN ISLANDS

The Ionian Sea, to the south of the Adriatic, between Italy and the west coast of Greece, is home to a delightful archipelago called the Ionian Islands. Covering 2,310sq km (892 square miles) of land, the primarily mountainous islands offer a dramatic landscape of rugged, vertiginous cliffs mixed with rolling hills and protected anchorages that provide a superb destination for cruising.

Just 70nm away from southern Italy, the islands are a popular destination for charter boats, yet despite a burgeoning tourist industry, there are still pockets of tranquillity to be found here, and the relatively sheltered waters offer excellent inter-island sailing.

The islands are the greenest of the Greek islands, and even in the summer remain lush and fertile, with many tiny villages backed by vast olive groves and vineyards. Historically, the Ionian Islands have had a chequered past, having been occupied by the Romans, Goths, Huns, Slavs, Patzinaks, Normans, Venetians and Ottoman Turks at various stages. This is reflected in their architecture, although much of the southern Ionian Islands were devastated in the 1953 earthquake.

Numerous harbours around the archipelago's main islands offer berths for visiting yachts, while many of the smaller islands are thickly populated with anchorages. And there is no shortage of places to eat, drink and restock either. Whether you spend a few weeks here or a whole season, there is plenty to explore, and the prevailing weather conditions are such that sailors of all abilities are guaranteed decent sailing.

below Navagio Beach on Zakynthos is typical of the white sand beaches and rugged cliffs of the Ionian Islands.

below The Laganas Gulf in Zakynthos is a good place to spot loggerhead turtles.

The route

Most cruises around the Ionian Islands start from Lefkada; however, those that would enjoy a longer passage between the islands should start from one of the northernmost islands such as Corfu, from where it is around 110nm to Zakynthos, the southernmost island.

The northern Ionian Islands offer slightly more challenging sailing than the southern islands, with less-protected waters, stronger winds and more shipping. Although parts of Corfu are heavily commercialized, the island of Paxos, just 7nm south of Corfu, is a real gem.

From there, head south towards Lefkada. On the way you could take a detour to explore the Amvrakikos Gulf immediately to the east of Preveza. This sizeable bay attracts over 250,000 birds from 250 species to its wetlands during the summer and is a real haven.

Continuing south, the next cluster of islands – Lefkada, Meganisi, Kalamos and Kastos – are at the heart of the Ionian Islands. It's the most sheltered part of the archipelago, and there are numerous places to visit packed into a relatively small area. If you are looking for choice, then this is the area to come.

The next island, Kefalonia, is the largest of the seven major Ionian Islands. Separated from Ithaca by a strait that is almost 2nm wide, it has comparatively few harbours and anchorages, but is a popular destination for its quintessential Greekness and its flourishing wine industry.

The southernmost island, and the last port of call before the Peloponnese, is Zakynthos. Known for its lush, verdant terrain, it is a popular tourist destination but an interesting place to explore nonetheless, with some stunningly beautiful bays and countryside.

Destinations

You really are spoilt for destinations in the Ionian Islands, as each of the seven major islands offer numerous places to explore.

Corfu: The second-largest island in the archipelago has been a popular tourist destination since the 1970s, but it is still possible to avoid the main hotspots and find some charming rural anchorages. Corfu Town is rich in history and is arguably the most beautiful town in the Ionian Islands, with evidence of its various occupiers visible in its architecture. In the North Corfu Channel, it's quieter, and you'll find one of the prettiest parts of the island, including the bays of Agios Stephanos and Kalami.

Paxos: A perfect antidote to the commerical tourism of Corfu, this island offers just three harbours, but all provide excellent shelter and reasonable facilities. The island is one of the most expensive parts of the area and popular with daytrippers, but it is still relatively unspoilt. Gaios, the southernmost harbour, fronted by beautiful Venetian architecture, is the most vibrant, while Lakka and Longos offer more traditional destinations.

Lefkada: This island lies to the south of Preveza and is an island of contrasts. Over 70 per cent of it is mountainous, yet long, sandy beaches fringe its north coast, steep craggy rocks dominate its western coast and pearly white cliffs loom over its south coast. Popular with Greek and Italian tourists, it offers both the commercialized ports of Nidri and Vasiliki – a windsurfer's Mecca – and more traditional harbours such as Sivota and Ligia.

Meganisi: One of the prettiest islands in the archipelago, Meganisi's deeply indented northern coastline gives good shelter in beautiful surroundings. There are five bays on this coast to choose from, but expect to meet lots of charter boats peak season as this is often their first port of call. Spilia Bay, with the village of Spartochori perched on the hillside above, is a

magical spot and despite its popularity remains relatively traditional.

Ithaca: Popular for its connections with Homer's *The Odyssey*, Ithaca is steep, barren and dramatic. The fjord-like Molos Gulf is home to the relatively uncommercialized Vathi, which has much to offer sailors, while Kioni consists of a cluster of Venetian-style buildings backed by thickly wooded olive groves.

Kefalonia: Devastated by the 1953 earthquake, in which 80 per cent of the island was razed, Kefalonia is mountainous and densely vegetated. It is one of the most distinctive islands, and Fiskardo on the northeastern tip is one of the most popular destinations. Well known for its wines and olive groves, it also offers quiet and unspoilt anchorages, and interesting places to visit inland.

Zakynthos: Stunning blue waters fringe Zakynthos, and while its rocky west coast has little to attract cruising yachts, more facilities are being made available on its eastern shores. The Blue Grotto of Korinthi, near Agios Nikolaos Bay, is stunning, as is the Laganas Gulf on the south coast. It is home to one of the only nesting sites of the loggerhead turtle in this region.

Level of skill

As a destination, the Ionian Islands are hard to beat, and they suit all abilities. The sailing is superb: predictable weather is combined with easy navigation, and there is a huge choice of harbours and anchorages available.

Distances between the main cluster of islands around Lefkada and Kefalonia are short too, so if you don't want to sail for hours at a time you don't have to. For those that want to be more adventurous, however, the northern and southern extremities of the Ionian Islands offer longer passages.

The winds among the islands are usually fairly predictable, and although during the summer there is little to no wind in the morning, by lunchtime a decent northwesterly Force 3–5 – the maistro – will invariably blow up, providing good sailing conditions for beginners and experienced sailors alike. Mid-summer, winds tend to be stronger, particularly in open stretches of water, and expect katabatic winds around the more mountainous areas during the evenings. The sirocco – a warm southwesterly or southeasterly wind that originates over Egypt and Libya – can also affect the area, particularly in the spring, and heavy swell can sometimes roll in.

Other hazards to note are the numerous rocks and reefs strewn around the islands' coasts, such as in the North Corfu Channel, off Paxos and between Skorpios and Meganisi. Most of the underlying rocks are easily visible on clear, calm days, but in choppy conditions when the seas are disturbed, they can be easily hidden. The waters are usually very busy with tripper boats and inter-island ferries too, and many of these travel at high speed so a good lookout needs to be maintained at all times. Fishing is also big business so be aware of fishing boats and fish farms, which are particularly prevalent in the bays off the mainland south of Preveza.

Berthing is generally stern- or bow-to pontoons, and most of the marinas and more popular harbours have lazylines rigged, which makes life easier.

When to go

The Ionian Islands generally enjoy a stable Mediterranean climate of hot summers and mild winters with a high average rainfall. Summer temperatures in this part of Greece tend to reach 28–32°C (82–90°F) during the day, cooler at night, but during the winter, temperatures can drop to as little as 15°C (29°F), with occasional snow on the mountains. The sailing season runs from May to early October and this is the best time to go, partly to enjoy the best of the weather, but also because during the winter and early spring most of the islands shut down completely. The islands can become very busy peak season, so it's worth considering visiting at the beginning or end of the season.

THE IONIAN ISLANDS AT A GLANCE

Route length: Approximately 110nm.

Time required: Two weeks would give you a whistle-stop tour of the Ionian Islands, but if you want to see more ashore, or visit more of the ports on the islands, then a month is ideal.

When to go: May to early October.

Weather: Generally stable, with hot summers, mild winters and predictable winds, although expect localized patterns between the islands: maistro in the afternoon and katabatic winds in the evenings.

Type and size of boat: Power or sail, ideally of around 25–45ft (7.6–13.7m). Some of the harbours/anchorages are quite small, so larger boats may struggle to find berthing/anchoring space.

Equipment: Depth sounder, chartplotter, decent anchor.

Tides: Tides and currents in the Ionian Sea are minimal, and are not a concern.

Hazards: Rocks and reefs, sandbanks, ferries and daytripper boats, fish farms, fishing boats and lobster pots.

Suitable for night sailing: Not recommended unless clear of the islands as many of the hazards mentioned above are unlit.

Difficulty of route: Easy to moderate.

Skills required: Basic navigation and ability to anchor and/or berth stern- or bow-to.

Charts: Imray: G11 (North Ionian Islands), G12 (South Ionian Islands), G121 (The Inland Sea). Admiralty: 5771 (Ionian Islands). Hellenic Navy Hydrographic Service: F21 (Ionian Sea Charts).

Berthing/mooring: Stern- or bow-to in most marinas with lazylines, and on some taverna-owned pontoons too. Otherwise anchoring offshore.

Ports of entry: Corfu Town (Corfu), Gaios (Paxos), Lefkada Town (Lefkada), Argostoli or Sami (Kefalonia), Vathi (Ithaca), Zakynthos Town (Zakynthos).

Water: Available throughout the Ionian Islands, although in shorter supply on the smaller islands such as Kalamos and Kastos.

Provisioning: Mini-markets can be found in most harbours, and some tavernas offer basic supplies. Most amenities can be found on larger islands.

Fuel: In the marinas and from local petrol stations (jerrycans).

Shorepower: Not widely available, except in marinas.

Maintenance: There are boatyards on the larger islands, and chandlers in Preveza, Lefkada Town and Zakynthos Town.

Family friendliness: This is a perfect area for cruising with the family.

Further reading: *Ionian Cruising Companion* by Vanessa Bird; *Ionian* by Rod Heikell.

left Distances between the main islands are small so you can easily travel between them.

VOYAGE 12

Turkey

THE AEGEAN COAST

If you are looking to cruise through ancient history, then Turkey is the place to do it. The Turkish coastline from Bodrum to Antalya oozes history and is an area that offers some of the most diverse and best preserved ancient ruins and sites of interest in Europe.

As a cruising ground this part of Turkey has much to offer, with a heavily indented coastline providing numerous bays in which to find secluded anchorages and traditional village harbours as well as lively resorts. Sailing here is delightful, with minimal navigational hazards, consistent winds and a huge choice of destinations. Although parts of the route are busy with tourists and popular with charter boats and daytrippers, other parts provide a view of a more traditional Turkey.

Historically, this area is particularly rich. Like Greece, Turkey has seen plenty of invaders. The Byzantines, Romans, Greeks and Persians have all set up camp here at one time or another and evidence of this abounds. If your interest is exploring ancient ruins you'll be spoilt for choice, and many of them lie within easy reach of the villages and harbours along this route.

Many boats choose to overwinter or base themselves along this coastline, and it's easy to see why, with continually improving facilities available, a delightful and extensive cruising area through stunning landscape and decent sailing conditions.

below Historical sites abound along this cruise, including the ancient castle at the entrance to Bodrum.

The route

This route covers around 250nm from Bodrum on the Carian coast, to Antalya, Turkey's biggest seaside resort. It's a linear cruise that can either stand alone in its own right or form part of a bigger cruise involving a circumnavigation of the Aegean Sea, calling in at Cyprus and Crete before heading west to the Peloponnese and the western shores of the Aegean.

From Bodrum the route heads east into Gökova Körfezi – a bay that stretches 40nm inland. Well protected by the Bodrum peninsula to the north and the Datça peninsula to the south, the bay's northern shore is of minimal interest but its southern coast is more attractive, with some delightful anchorages. The charming Değirmen Bükü, a forest-lined bay in the southeastern corner, is definitely worth a visit, as is Kara Ada, an island immediately south of Bodrum town, despite its popularity with daytrippers.

Next, head southwest to Knidos on the western tip of the Datça peninsula, before making the short hop to the next destination at Hayıt Bükü, a sheltered bay well stocked with good restaurants. You can then head on to Datça, 10nm farther to the east. Other destinations within the Hisarönü Körfezi, on which Datça stands, include Keçi Bükü (Orhaniye), 20nm to the west, where there is a good marina (Marti Marina) and anchorages. Bozburun, to the southwest offers more facilities for yachts and is a cheaper alternative to Marmaris, the next port of call on this route.

Heading east from Marmaris, the coastline is dominated by pine-forested mountains and offers a number of destinations. Popular with charter fleets, the 180nm stretch to Antalya can get busy, so be prepared to anchor in company. Ekincik Bükü is a popular place to stay overnight, while Göcek at the northern end of Skopea Limani will provide most facilities, as will Fethiye on the other side of the bay. From here, head to the harbours of Kalkan and then Kaş farther to the east, before another 15nm hop to the bay at Kekova Roads, and finally Antalya.

below Fethiye Harbour is a pleasant alternative anchorage to Göcek.

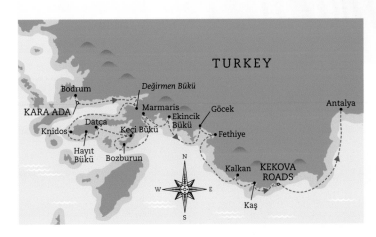

Destinations

Bodrum: This city is a major yachting and tourist destination. It is busy, but is delightful too, having a real buzz about it. Gulets and yachts vie for space in the northern part of the harbour, but Mita Marina on the western side is a good place to restock and replenish before starting a cruise. The city itself is packed with things to do and see, including the Museum of Underwater Archaeology at the Castle of St Peter, Turkish baths (*hamams*), the Mausoleum from c.350BCE and the ruins of a shipyard where much of the Ottoman fleet was rebuilt in the 18th century after it was destroyed in 1770 by the Russians.

Kara Ada: A popular destination with daytrippers out of Bodrum, this island lies 3nm south of the city and has three anchorages. Ashore you'll find the island's famous healing hot springs as well as caves and a restaurant.

Değirmen Bükü: Lying at the eastern end of Gökova Körfezi bay, this forested inlet is also known as the English Harbour after it was used by the British Special Boat Service (SBS) as a base for torpedo boats during World War II. There are several restaurants here, plus good walks through the pine forests.

Knidos: The ruins at Knidos make this a popular destination. The harbour itself has room for visiting yachts and there is also an anchorage. The ruins, which sit on the hillside above the harbour, were originally used by the Ancient Greeks for festivals to honour their gods, including Apollo and Poseidon.

Marmaris: The resort town of Marmaris lies 40nm from Bodrum and is a thriving yachting centre and tourist destination. Set in a beautiful and sheltered location, it is home to several marinas and is a good place to do some shopping.

Göcek: This coastline has plenty of marinas and facilities for yachts, and at Göcek there are six marinas to choose from. The town, which lies at the northern end of Skopea Limani bay, has a regular street market and is a popular destination with cruising yachts.

Fethiye: Standing on the other side of the bay from Göcek, Fethiye is built on the ancient site of the city of Telmessos. The town offers a marina and boatyards, and yachts can anchor in the northeastern corner of the bay to the west of the island of Fethiye Ad.

Kalkan: This small harbour was once popular with charter fleets but is now much quieter, and there is usually room to berth. It is a pretty town to visit with some good restaurants and a relaxed atmosphere.

Kaş: Lying 12nm east of Kalkan and 12nm west of Kekova Roads, Kaş is a delightful little town, full of narrow, winding streets and surrounded by archaeological sites of interest. A marina was opened in 2011 that also provides full boatyard services.

Antalya: Tourism is big business in this city, which is also known as the 'Turkish Riviera'. Although visiting boats can no longer berth in the medieval harbour in the centre, they can moor in Celebi Marina to the east. Ashore you will find a number of sites of interest. The old town, Kaleiçi, is packed with cobbled streets and historic buildings, protected by the medieval stone walls that encircle it. Hadrian's Gate and the Kaleiçi Museum are worth a visit, as is the Antalya Archaeological Museum and its collection of artefacts from the region.

Level of skill

There are no particular skills required for this route. Most of the pilotage involves eyeball navigation, and generally ports, anchorages and islands can be easily identified. Tidal ranges in this part of the Mediterranean are minimal and the route is reasonably hazard-free. Watch out for strong currents around the Bodrum and Datça peninsulas, as well as isolated unmarked rocks close inshore.

The northwesterly meltemi, which blows across this region from mainland Greece to Turkey between May and October, can cause strong winds (often reaching Force 6–7) in the afternoon, particularly around Bodrum and Knidos. Some of the areas in the east where steep mountains lead down to the shoreline can also be particularly gusty and squally close in. Swell is an occasional side effect of the meltemi.

The biggest skill that is required within this area, and indeed much of the Mediterranean, is berthing stern- or bow-to. Many of the harbours within this route are small, and space is at a premium, so to fit as many boats in as possible most harbours encourage stern-or bow-to berthing.

Anchorages can get crowded too, as many of the bays are very deep until close in, which reduces the amount of available space. Anchoring off in depths of up to 52m is not unusual, and it is good practice to take a stern line ashore and attach it to a rock or tree for added security. This will prevent your boat from swinging round its anchor and bumping into other boats in crowded bays.

When to go

One of the many attractions of cruising in Turkey is the length of the sailing season. Although winters in this area tend to be wet and mild, they are also short, so the sailing season is longer. From late April onwards the rain stops and temperatures start to rise, and until about late October conditions are usually very settled. Expect extreme temperatures in July and August, sometimes rising to 38°C (100°F)-plus.

Winds in this area are fairly consistent – varying from northwesterly through to northerly and generally Force 3–4. Around the Bodrum peninsula they are slightly stronger at Force 4–5, but the farther east you go the weaker they become. The meltemi can produce strong Force 6–7 winds, and localized squalls are not unusual in bays flanked by steep-sided mountains.

THE AEGEAN COAST AT A GLANCE

Route length: Around 250nm.

Time required: Allow three to four weeks, more if you want to do more exploring ashore.

When to go: Late April to late October.

Weather: Coastal Mediterranean climate: hot and dry summers and wet and mild winters. Northwesterly Force 3–5 winds are the norm.

Type and size of boat: Power or sail, 25ft (7.6m) plus.

Equipment: No specific equipment, other than basic navigational equipment and anchoring gear. A bimini is very useful during the hot summers.

Tides: Minimal tidal range.

Hazards: Some strong currents around the headlands off Bodrum and Datça, and you should keep an eye out for isolated rocks when navigating close inshore, and fishing boats too.

Suitable for night sailing: Yes.

Difficulty of route: Easy to moderate.

Skills required: Berthing stern- and bow-to.

Charts: Imray: G35 (Dodecanese and the Coast of Turkey), G36 (Marmaris to Geyikova Adasi), G40 (Kaş to Antalya), M21 (South coast of Turkey; Syria; Lebanon; Cyprus). Admiralty: 236 (Nísos Ródhos to Taslik Burnu), 1099 (East Approaches to Aegean Sea), 1055 (Rhodes Channel and Gökova Körfezi), 1054 (Marmaris to Kaş), 237 (Taslik Burnu to Anamur Burnu).

Berthing/mooring: Most marinas offer stern- or bow-to berthing. Anchoring opportunities are limited too, as many of the bays are deep until very close inshore, so expect to anchor in close proximity to other boats.

Ports of entry: Bodrum, Datça, Marmaris, Fethiye, Kas, Antalya.

Water: Fresh water is available at most ports and at all marinas. You will need your own hose, though, and at some places water is metered, so don't get caught out if you are asked to pay for it.

Provisioning: Small shops and mini-markets in most of the harbours and marinas.

Fuel: Bottled gas is widely available from marinas and at mini-markets. Check that your gas regulator is compatible, though, as Turkish regulators differ from those used in other parts of Europe. Diesel and petrol are readily available from marinas/local petrol stations.

Shorepower: Available at most marinas and the larger harbours along the route.

Maintenance: Available at most marinas along the route.

Family friendliness: Very family friendly. Lots of beaches and shoreside activities and the locals are very welcoming.

Further reading: *Turkey Cruising Companion* by Emma Watson; *Turkish Waters & Cyprus Pilot* by Rod and Lucinda Heikell; *Magic Turkey* by Alfredo Giacon; *Cruise the Black Sea* by Doreen and Archie Annan.

left The ancient Greek ruins at Knidos sit above the harbour and make a fascinating visit.

VOYAGE 13

The Atlantic Ocean

TRANSATLANTIC CROSSING

Every year, around 4,000 to 5,000 people sail across the Atlantic, bound either for the Caribbean or, if coming west to east, the Mediterranean and Europe. For many, it's purely a delivery trip, a one-way cruise to open up new and unexplored waters; for others, it's the adventure of a lifetime – the achievement of crossing a great expanse of water, and being out of sight of land for several weeks, while being totally self-sufficient.

Whatever your reason for making the crossing, the experience is unique. No two crossings are ever the same, and while it can be a lonely and desolate place to be if you experience problems on board or heavy weather, it can also be a magical place. There is something deeply humbling about being in the middle of an ocean, with water as far as the eye can see, and no other boats, as well as a vast night's sky that is illuminated by an infinite number of twinkling stars and no man-made light pollution.

As modern cruising boats have become more efficient through the water, so crossing times have decreased and most transatlantics from the Canary Islands to the Caribbean now take between three and four weeks, depending on weather conditions. There is no 'definitive' boat in which to cross the Atlantic either, and indeed in 1993 solo sailor Hugo Vihlen made the crossing in *Father's Day*, a boat that measured just 5ft 4in (1.6m) in length! You must, however, be very well prepared to ensure your cruise is as enjoyable as it can be.

below No two crossings of the Atlantic are ever the same, but for it to be successful, preparation is the key.

The route

For many people, the start of a transatlantic begins in the Canary Islands, a group of 13 islands located 54nm off the northwest coast of Africa. Of these Gran Canaria, the third largest, is a favourite with west-bound yachtsmen.

Many events such as the Atlantic Rally for Cruisers (ARC), in which over 200 yachts make the crossing together, start from here. It's a good place to prepare, with excellent facilities available at Las Palmas de Gran Canaria Marina.

Although a more northerly crossing will involve a shorter distance, and therefore less time, a crossing that starts farther south is often considered a better option because you get a better angle to the trade winds for the crossing and are less likely to encounter hurricanes. Christopher Columbus made his second transatlantic

crossing from the Canary Islands in 1493, and today most yachts crossing from here head southwest until around 20°N 30°W before turning west towards the Caribbean.

Alternatively, you can head initially on a more south-southwesterly bearing, which will take you relatively close to the Cape Verde Islands, providing an optional landfall should you need to reprovision or make repairs before heading west. This route is longer, but if time is not an option, may be worth considering. In total, the route from Las Palmas to Rodney Bay on St Lucia in the Lesser Antilles via a latitude of 20°N 30°W is around 2,433nm.

below Marinas on St Lucia can get busy but Marigot Bay on the west coast offers a quieter place to anchor.

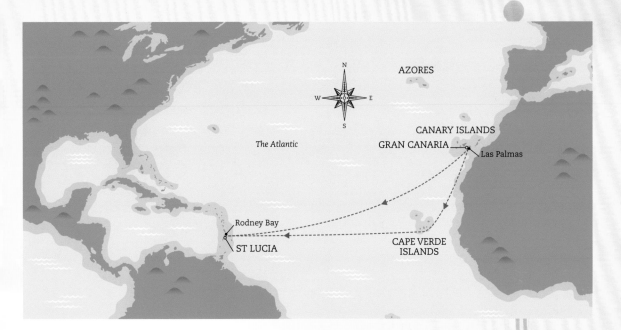

Destinations

Gran Canaria: As a place to start your transatlantic adventure, Gran Canaria is hard to beat. The island is the third biggest in the archipelago and the second most populated, as well as a popular destination for many holidaymakers from around the world. For many cruising yachts the island is merely a stopover; however, the Canary Islands themselves offer an interesting cruising destination in their own right.

The main destination for transatlantic-bound yachts on Gran Canaria is Las Palmas, with its excellent marina. Located on the northeast corner of the island, this city has everything you need, including food supplies, while equipment or services are all within easy reach. Expect it to be busy in November, as this is the time when the annual Atlantic Rally for Cruisers makes its departure for St Lucia.

Gran Canaria is beautiful and diverse and has much to offer if you have the time to explore it. There are traditional villages and towns, beaches galore and the usual tourist attractions, but the cave systems at the archaeological sites of Cenobio de Valerón and La Cueva Pintada and the Jardin Canario botanical gardens are especially well worth a visit.

St Lucia: With its spectacular volcanic mountains, the 616sq km (238 square mile) island of St Lucia is part of the Lesser Antilles chain, which lies on the eastern side of the Caribbean Sea. Situated 44nm north of St Vincent and the same distance south of Martinique, much of the island is thick with lush rainforest vegetation and mountains, but it is an excellent landfall for yachts heading westbound across the Atlantic.

Rodney Bay, on the northern shore of St Lucia, is the first port of call for most yachts visiting the island. Its marina, which can accommodate boats up to 285ft (86.9m) in length, is now one of the most popular in this part of the Caribbean. Consequently it does get busy in peak season – particularly with superyachts – so if you are looking for quieter places head south along St Lucia's west coast and anchor or berth in Marigot Bay. This attractive bay is home to a charter fleet, but some facilities are also available to visiting yachts. Alternatively, Soufrière and Vieux Fort farther to the south also offer limited services.

Ashore there is plenty to do, including tours to the Diamond Waterfalls and Botanical Gardens, Sulphur Springs, Fond Doux cacao bean plantation and the Pigeon Island National Park.

Level of skill

You don't need a Yachtmaster qualification to cross the Atlantic, but it helps. What is crucial, however, is an ability to be self-sufficient, and a thorough knowledge of your boat and all the systems on board. Hundreds of miles offshore you need to be able to cope with whatever nature throws at you. If that's calm weather, then an ability to keep the boat moving is important, but knowing how to tackle heavy weather conditions is even more crucial.

Questions to ask yourself prior to making a crossing are:

- Do you have the seamanship skills to know how to shorten sail and batten down the hatches so that the boat and all its crew are safe in bad weather?
- Have you got the practical ability to effect repairs and carry out maintenance should parts of the boat fail?

The major difference between offshore and coastal sailing is that with the latter, if there is a problem, the chances are you are relatively close to a harbour or port in which to seek refuge and help, or within range of the rescue services. But if you develop a problem with your rigging, rudder or autopilot in the mid-Atlantic, then it is up to you to fix it. Long-distance sailing places incredible strains on a boat, and the chances are gear will fail, so carry plenty of spares and repair manuals.

Electronic gizmos can be very useful, but there is a lot to be said for keeping onboard systems simple.

Electronics require a huge amount of energy to power them. The marine environment can also be hostile for electronics, with salt water being particularly corrosive.

As most of the cruise is offshore, the pilotage skills needed are fairly minimal, but you will need good navigation skills. Having some knowledge of using a sextant, and being able to plot your position by dead reckoning (DR) or running fix (RF) is also essential rather than relying totally on GPS and chartplotters.

A strong crew with plenty of hands on board will break the monotony of endless days at sea, help solve problems, or steer if your autopilot fails.

When to go

Most people make the crossing from the Canary Islands to the Lesser Antilles in November/December. The hurricane season in the Caribbean, which runs from 1 June to 30 November, will be just ending, and you will reach your destination at the start of the sailing season there. By late November you will also encounter lighter winds around the Canary Islands, while temperatures are typically around 19–21°C (66–69°F). In the mid-Atlantic the trade winds have usually also established themselves by then. If you can find them, they will provide a sleigh-ride to your destination.

At this time of year expect wind conditions in the Atlantic to be around Force 4–6, with a rolling, steady swell, but also expect the unexpected. Weather in the Atlantic is often changeable and unpredictable, and while for some people crossing at this time of year conditions may be perfect, others may encounter squalls, cross swells or periods of calm.

Lying close to the Equator, St Lucia has average temperatures of around 29°C (84°F) throughout the year, and is controlled by the northeasterly trade winds. It is usually dry between December and May, with any rainfall coinciding with the hurricane season.

TRANSATLANTIC CROSSING AT A GLANCE

Route length: Around 2,433nm.

Time required: Allow at least three to four weeks.

When to go: Time your arrival in the Caribbean with the start of the sailing season there, so aim to leave Gran Canaria in November/December. Avoid the hurricane season, from June to November.

Weather: Gran Canaria's climate is subtropical. Northeasterly winds prevail and are at their strongest during the summer months. St Lucia has a stable climate. The rainy season runs from June to November and the dry season from December to May. Temperatures average 29°C (84°F).

Type and size of boat: 24ft (7.3m) is considered the minimum length. Most modern production yachts will cope well with a transatlantic run, although you may need to upgrade systems and equipment. Large boats can feel more stable, but require big crews and good energy sources.

Equipment: GPS, chartplotter, radar, Navtex, Inmarsat, SSB radio, liferaft, lifejackets and harnesses for all crew, EPIRB (Emergency Position Indicating Radio Beacon), PLBs (Personal Locator Beacons), flares, first-aid kit, repair manuals, watermaker and plenty of spares.

Hazards: Shipping, semi-submerged containers and other floating debris, heavy weather.

Suitable for night sailing: Night sailing is unavoidable but the mid-Atlantic is a wonderful place to experience incredible night skies.

Difficulty of route: Medium to hard.

Skills required: Good boat handling skills, self-sufficiency, first-aid and heavy weather sailing. Excellent maintenance and repair skills and knowledge of sextant and plotting by DR or RF.

Charts: Imray: E2 (Islas Canarias), 100 (North Atlantic Ocean Passage Chart). Admiralty: 4004 (North Atlantic Ocean and the Mediterranean Sea), 5124 (Routeing Chart North Atlantic Ocean). Atlantic Pilot Atlas (Adlard Coles Nautical).

Berthing/mooring: Gran Canaria: Las Palmas de Gran Canaria Marina, Anfi Del Mar Marina, Puerto Rico Marina. St Lucia: Rodney Bay Marina.

Ports of entry: Rodney Bay, Castries, Marigot Bay and Vieux Fort in St Lucia.

Water: It is a good idea to install a watermaker to produce your own drinking water, but fresh water can be supplied from provisioning locations.

Provisioning: Gran Canaria: Las Palmas de Gran Canaria Marina, Anfi Del Mar Marina, Puerto Rico Marina. St Lucia: Rodney Bay Marina and Marigot Bay. Fresh produce will not last long in hot climates. A store of tinned food is good, but vacuum-packed food is lighter and takes up less space.

Fuel: Supplied from the same locations as for provisioning. Renewable power sources, such as wind and sun, will help top up your batteries.

Shorepower: Las Palmas and Rodney Bay Marina.

Maintenance: Most services can be found at Las Palmas and at Rodney Bay Marina. Some services can also be found at Marigot Bay.

Family friendliness: You need to be able to amuse your children for weeks on end, within the confines of a boat and without shoreside comforts.

Further reading: *World Cruising Routes* by Jimmy Cornell; *Sailing an Atlantic Circuit/Atlantic Sailors' Handbook* by Alastair Buchan; *Your First Atlantic Crossing* by Les Weatheritt; *Atlantic Crossing Guide* by RCC Pilotage Foundation.

VOYAGE 14
The Caribbean

ST VINCENT AND THE GRENADINES
Thirty-two volcanic islands form the Caribbean territory of St Vincent and the Grenadines. Of these, ten provide the main focal point for anyone cruising this area and they offer some of the most stunning sailing in the Lesser Antilles.

Less developed than many of the islands in the Caribbean, St Vincent and the Grenadines form the southern half of the Windward Islands, which extend from Dominica in the north to Grenada in the south. The archipelago, which lies 40nm south of St Lucia, stretches for around 60nm, with its two primary destinations, St Vincent and Union Island, bookmarking each end of the group.

Sailing here is fabulous. Stable weather patterns and constant winds during the summer season produce ideal conditions. With clear blue skies, turquoise waters, tropical white-sand beaches and sheltered anchorages, it's not hard to see why this is one of the most popular destinations in the world for cruising.

Despite its popularity this area hasn't really been spoilt and hasn't changed too much either, so you still get a flavour of how the Caribbean used to be. Tourism is big business here, but not at the detriment of the local environment. Unlike other territories within the Caribbean, jet-skis and wave-runners are banned within these waters and conservation is at the forefront of island life. Wander ashore and you'll discover totally unspoiled areas, while the 2nm-long reef system and marine park of the Tobago Cays is a diver's paradise.

below Despite the fabulous sailing conditions, the Lesser Antilles have remained remarkably unspoilt.

The route

This route is a circular route of around 120nm, and runs the length of the island chain and back. The start and end destination is Blue Lagoon on St Vincent, the most northerly island in the archipelago. Blue Lagoon is the island's main charter base, and a good place at which to restock and replenish before heading south, owing to its location near Kingstown, St Vincent's capital. Alternatively, an anchorage off Young Island, a small resort island off the southern coast of St Vincent near Kingstown, provides a good introduction to the archipelago.

From here, head due south to Bequia, the largest island in the Grenadines. You can either anchor in the wonderfully sheltered Admiralty Bay on the island's leeward shore, or visit the equally attractive harbour town of Port Elizabeth. Friendship Bay on the southern coast of the island provides an alternative place to stay overnight. The route then continues 14nm south-southeast to Mustique, one of the gems of this cruise, and Britannia Bay, the island's main destination. No anchoring is allowed off Mustique – visitors must pick up a mooring.

Head another 18nm southwest and you'll reach Tobago Cays Marine Park, passing en route to starboard the island of Canouan. From Tobago Cays, the route continues south-southwest to Petit St Vincent. You can make a diversion here to visit the island of Carriacou, or continue farther southwest to Grenada. Alternatively, head northwest to Union Island and then northeast to the island of Mayreau with its delightful anchorages, 4nm west of Tobago Cays. It is then another 7nm north-northwest to Canouan before returning to Bequia and finally St Vincent.

below Tobago Cays has a spectacular marine park, which is one of the main attractions of the area.

Destinations

St Vincent: The administrative capital of the northern Grenadines, St Vincent is the biggest island in the group at 345sq km (133 square miles) and is largely unspoilt. The leeward coast offers numerous sheltered anchorages, while ashore you'll find a variety of things to see and do. The volcano La Soufrière is classed as active (although the last eruption was in 1979) and forms a focal point on the northern part of the island. There are many good walks around its base and peak. Elsewhere, the Falls of Baleine on the north coast or the Botanical Gardens near Kingstown are worth a visit too.

Bequia: Admiralty Bay on the island's leeward shore forms the main focus of attention for cruisers. This large, natural bay offers splendid anchorages, while in Port Elizabeth you'll find a good selection of shops, restaurants and bars, as well as an opportunity to explore the island's boatbuilding and whaling heritage.

Mustique: Lying 14nm south of Bequia, the island of Mustique is privately owned and mainly inhabited by the rich and famous. Measuring 5.5sq km (2.1 square miles), the island's main port of call is within Britannia Bay. Anchoring off Mustique is not permitted, but visitors may pick up a mooring within the bay and take their dinghy ashore. Here you'll find basic provisions, bars and restaurants, and some good walking trails.

Tobago Cays: This group of islands and the Horseshoe Reef that encircles it is the main reason why most people visit the Grenadines. This huge marine park is simply stunning and is home to a fascinating underwater world filled with a vast array of species. Lying 18nm south of Mustique, the five uninhabited islets are relatively unspoilt, and visitors can either pick up a mooring or anchor in the designated locations within the lagoon. Tobago Cays was the location for two of the *Pirates of the Caribbean* films.

Union Island: Clifton Harbour on the east coast is the main destination on Union Island, and here you will find various shops, restaurants and bars. Alternatively, head for Chatham Bay on the western side of the island, which is fringed by a wonderful crescent-shaped beach. The airport on the east coast of the island is a prominent landmark, as is the distinctive Mount Taboi to the west. Hiking trails up the latter can be explored, while the former provides good links for exchanges of crew. There is also an anchorage off Frigate Island to the south.

Mayreau: Another gem on this route lies 4nm to the west of Tobago Cays. Saltwhistle Bay on the north coast of Mayreau is a firm favourite with cruising boats and provides good holding in a sheltered anchorage. During peak season it is usually crammed full, but an alternative anchorage can be found in Saline Bay on the west coast. Ashore you'll find good walks between the two bays, as well as a resort that welcomes visiting sailors.

Level of skill

Sailing around St Vincent and the Grenadines is fabulous, but you need a certain amount of experience to enjoy it to the full. Although the islands are within easy reach of each other and relatively easy to identify, some of the passages are in open water and out of the shelter of the islands. Weather conditions tend to be fairly settled here, with the prevailing winds from the northeast and speeds of between 15–25 knots; however, it can be challenging at times.

Currents in this area flow from north to south, so for the first half of the passage you will enjoy a sleigh-ride journey. Some can be quite strong, though, so watch out for leeway. Returning home to St Vincent from Union Island, however, it is a bit more of an uphill journey, so be prepared for swell and wind on the nose.

Hazards to be aware of are primarily reefs and isolated rocks near the islands. The water is very clear in this area, so if a good lookout is maintained they can usually be spotted in advance. However, take particular care around Tobago Cays. There are designated anchoring zones here, which are strictly enforced so as to protect the marine park from damage. It is also useful to have good practical experience of anchoring.

Unfortunately, as tourism increases so too do the number of thefts taking place from boats, and sadly St Vincent and the Grenadines is not immune to this. Some of these have been reportedly quite violent, so caution should be exercised, and you are advised to lock your boat up securely when going ashore. The very useful cruising website *www.noonsite.com* has more details on crime in the area and places to avoid.

When to go

St Vincent and the Grenadines get the full benefit of the easterly trade winds. During the traditional Caribbean sailing season, which runs from December through to May, the islands experience very settled conditions. Winds in this area usually blow 15–25 knots from the northeast at this time of year, with average temperatures of 29°C (84°F). Showers are frequent but rarely long-lasting in the dry season, whereas the rainy season that runs from May to December can involve reasonable downfalls. July is notoriously wet, although temperatures remain high, resulting in high humidity. Lying so far south, however, the islands are right on the edge of the hurricane belt and consequently are little affected by them. In fact the last recorded hurricane to hit was in 1955.

As would be expected, during peak season St Vincent and the Grenadines get very popular with visiting boats. It pays to arrive either early or late in the season if you want to explore the islands without too many other people around.

ST VINCENT AND THE GRENADINES AT A GLANCE

Route length: Around 120nm, depending on which islands you visit and whether you include a detour to Grenada.

Time required: Two to three weeks.

When to go: December to May.

Weather: Tropical climate. December to May average temperatures of 29°C (84°F), with short and sharp showers, but plenty of sunshine.

Type and size of boat: Power or sail, 25ft (7.6m) plus.

Equipment: Charts, chartplotter, depth sounder, binoculars, bimini.

Tides: Tidal range within the islands is around 46cm. Currents can run quite quickly.

Hazards: Reefs and isolated rocks, strong currents and busy anchorages.

Suitable for night sailing: The presence of reefs can make this hazardous, but entry to some of the bigger islands is possible.

Difficulty of route: Moderate.

Skills required: Basic navigation, ability to maintain a good lookout, good boat handling skills, anchoring experience.

Charts: Imray: B3 (The Grenadines), B311 (Middle Grenadines), B31 (Grenadines – Middle Sheet), B30 (Grenadines – North Sheet). Admiralty: 795 (The Grenadines – Southern Part), 794 (The Grenadines – Central Part), 793 (The Grenadines – Northern Part).

Berthing/mooring: St Vincent: Blue Lagoon, Ottley Hall Marina; Bequia: mooring buoys and marina at Port Elizabeth; Mustique: mooring buoys in Britannia Bay; Tobago Cays: 30 mooring buoys; Union Island: stern-to berths at Anchorage Bay YC. Numerous anchorages exist throughout the archipelago.

Ports of entry: Kingstown on St Vincent, Bequia, Union Island.

Water: Available at most of the main destinations. Avoid drinking tap water, however.

Provisioning: Available at most of the main destinations on the route.

Fuel: Available at Blue Lagoon on St Vincent, Port Elizabeth on Bequia.

Shorepower: Minimal availability.

Maintenance: Available at Blue Lagoon and Ottley Hall Marina on St Vincent, Port Elizabeth on Bequia.

Family friendliness: Very family friendly. However, the islands have seen an increase in thefts from boats in recent years, so exercise some caution.

Further reading: *Windward Anchorages* by Chris Doyle; *Sailor's Guide to the Windward Islands* by Chris Doyle.

VOYAGE 15

The Caribbean

THE BRITISH VIRGIN ISLANDS

It's not hard to see why the British Virgin Islands (BVIs) are now the most popular destination in the world for charter companies. The combination of azure blue, crystal-clear waters, iridescent white sandy beaches, excellent facilities and steady trade-wind sailing is a powerful one, and one that attracts thousands of sailors to the archipelago's shores each year.

Quiet it is not, particularly peak season, when the chances of getting a secluded cove to yourself are rare, but do not let this put you off. The sailing is so superb that it's easy to forgive the masses for joining you, and while some of the more popular anchorages are often packed with boats of all shapes and sizes, it's still possible to find quieter areas and unspoiled places ashore teeming with a diverse array of wildlife.

It was the South American Arawaks who first colonized the islands in around 100BCE but it wasn't until 1493, when the Carib tribe occupied the islands, that they were first seen by European eyes. Having embarked on his second voyage of discovery in October 1493, Christopher Columbus identified the islands later that year – naming them the Islas de Santa Úrsula y las Once Mil Vírgenes, after Saint Ursula and the 11,000 virgins who followed her – as well as the islands of Tortola, Virgin Gorda and Peter Island.

In total there are around 50 islands and islets to explore within the archipelago, some inhabited, others not. And if you want to extend the cruise further, the US Virgin Islands – St John, St Thomas and St Croix – are just to the west and south.

below The island of Virgin Gorda is famous for its massive granite boulders, popular with both scuba divers and beach-goers.

The route

This route follows a clockwise circumnavigation of the BVIs. It begins and ends at Road Town on Tortola, the main port within the island group. Although this destination is not the most charming, being a major port for cruise ships and superyachts, it is a great place to provision and stock up before exploring the rest of the archipelago.

From here, head southeast for around 7nm to Cooper Island, where a good anchorage can be found on the west coast of the island. It is then a short hop to Salt Island, before the route continues southeast to Peter Island and either Sprat Bay or Great Harbour. Immediately to the southeast of Peter Island lies Norman Island, the next destination, which has a good anchorage in The Bight bay, before the route continues for around 11nm northwest between Flanagan Island and The Indians, along the northeast coast of St John and into West End bay on Tortola, which is tucked behind Frenchman's Cay.

From here, follow the coast round the southwestern tip of Tortola, passing through the channel between Great Thatch Island and Tortola, before heading north-northwest to Jost Van Dyke. White Bay on the southeast coast of the island is a definite place to visit, but the nearby Great Harbour and Diamond Cay, on the island's east coast, are also worth exploring.

It is then a 7nm sail back to Cane Garden Bay on the northwest coast of Tortola. From here, follow the coast round, past the private Guana Island and Little Camanoe before arriving at Marina Cay, a small island just off Great Camanoe. For those with more experience, you can then head east and then northeast for around 22nm to Anegada, or alternatively, head directly for the north coast of Virgin Gorda, 9nm to the east-northeast.

North Sound and the Bitter End Yacht Club is worth a visit, before the route heads southwest to Spanish Town, the island's main port. A visit to The Baths National Park on the southern tip of Virgin Gorda is also recommended, and from here it is about a 10nm sail back to Road Town on Tortola.

below Marina Cay is a beautiful small island near to Great Camanoe and well worth a visit.

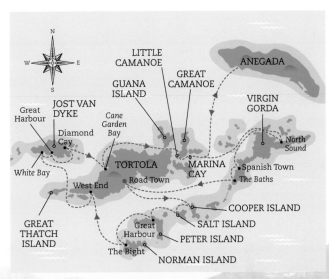

Destinations

Tortola: Tortola is the largest island within the archipelago and the most heavily developed too. Road Town, with its large harbour, lies in the centre of the south coast, and it is here that many of the boating facilities are based. A busy port with cruise ships, it is a good place to provision and start a cruise, although often packed with tourists. Other destinations on the island include Soper's Hole, tucked in West End behind Frenchman's Cay, and the delightful Cane Garden Bay, a wide, expansive bay offering good shelter on the island's northwest coast.

Salt Island: Named after the salt ponds that cover much of its interior, Salt Island is a very tranquil place to visit. Less popular ashore with tourists than the other islands in this chain, it is home to just a few people and a few derelict houses. The island is also notorious for the RMS *Rhone*, the Royal Mail packet steamer that sank off its shores during a hurricane in 1867. It is now a popular dive site, and one of the best in the Caribbean.

Jost Van Dyke: No visit to Jost Van Dyke is complete without a trip to White Bay and the famous Soggy Dollar Bar, home of the even more famous Painkiller cocktail. The bar was set up on the beach in the 1970s and at that time the only way of accessing it was via the sea, with patrons swimming ashore and paying for their drinks with soggy dollars. White Bay lives up to its name with its incredibly white sand and is a great spot to enjoy a rum-based Painkiller or two, while Diamond Cay on the east coast of the island is another alternative. The National Park lies off Long Bay on Jost Van Dyke and several daytime anchorages provide the opportunity to see the cay's bird sanctuary.

Virgin Gorda: The shape of this island is said to resemble a woman lying on her side, and Columbus is said to have named it Virgin Gorda (Fat Virgin) for that

very reason. The third largest island in the archipelago, it lies to the east of Tortola and offers several good anchorages and marinas. To the south are The Baths, a world-famous collection of massive granite boulders on the beach that are popular with beach-goers and scuba divers alike. On the north coast, in the North Sound, near Prickly Pear Island, is the Bitter End Yacht Club with a full-service marina and excellent facilities. There is also a superyacht marina within Leverick Bay to the west. Spanish Town, the island's capital, lies on the west coast and this is a good destination if you need to restock with provisions.

Anegada: If you make the passage to Anegada you won't be disappointed. This low-lying island is one of the most stunning in the archipelago. Loblolly Bay on its north coast offers one of the finest beaches in the Caribbean, although it is not possible to anchor near to it; there is just one anchorage on the south coast. Taxis or jeeps can be easily hired to make the short passage across the island. On the way, cast your eye towards the salt ponds on the western side of the island and you may spot flocks of flamingos. The Horseshoe Reef, which extends southeastwards, is the largest barrier reef in the Caribbean. It is also one of the most notorious, being the graveyard of numerous ships, including the Royal Navy's 32-ton frigate HMS *Astraea* in 1808.

Level of skill

The beauty of the BVIs is that it's not an area restricted to sailors with a lot of experience. The cruising ground here is protected and relatively sheltered, which means that the sailing is not too challenging, but instead consistently good, with the steady easterly trade winds producing ideal passage-making conditions.

The wind can pick up at times, but this route is relatively hazard-free. The navigation is all by eyeball. Most of the bays are deep and unlike many other archipelagos around the world there aren't too many unmarked reefs and rocks to avoid. Those that there are are clearly marked, or easy to avoid, and with the islands all within close reach of each other you don't have to make long, arduous passages if you don't want to.

There is only one island that poses potential difficulties for novice crews, and indeed many charter companies will not allow their customers to visit it, unless skippered or led by a guide. Anegada, the most northerly of the BVIs, is the real gem of the archipelago. Unspoiled, the island is distinct for its topographical uniqueness. The rest of the BVIs are formed of lofty peaks, and are densely vegetated. Anegada in contrast is low-lying, so low-lying in fact that it stands just 8.5m (28ft) above sea level and isn't visible until very close in. It is surrounded by a reef, which includes the notorious Horseshoe Reef on its southeastern corner. Approach to the island must only be made in the most settled of conditions, as the coral heads that fringe it make arrival at the island's only anchorage a particularly hazardous

task unless you stick to the carefully marked channel. Leave your port of departure early in the morning to ensure good visibility and a mooring or space to anchor, and do not on any account attempt an approach at night.

When to go

The sailing season in the BVIs runs from December to May, with the busiest months being December through to early March. To avoid the crowds, aim to visit from late March through to May, although even then it can still get busy. Temperatures during the season are relatively stable, with average highs of 27–31°C (81–88°F), but it has been known to rise as high as 35°C (95°F) in April.

Wind conditions are wonderfully stable thanks to the easterly trade winds, with steady 15–25-knot northeasterlies blowing in the winter months and 10–15-knot southeasterlies blowing in the summer months. It can get boisterous at times, with winds picking up in the afternoons, but rarely is it too windy for most people to enjoy. However, avoid visiting between June and November, as the archipelago lies within the hurricane belt and conditions here have been known to get very unpleasant indeed.

August to December are typically the wettest months, coinciding with the hurricane season, although May can also be wet. Expect heavy downpours during the season, although most are short-lived and often over as soon as they begin.

THE BRITISH VIRGIN ISLANDS AT A GLANCE

Route length: Around 110nm.

Time required: At least two weeks.

When to go: December to May.

Weather: Tropical climate, with average highs of 27–31°C (81–88°F) between December and May. It has consistent 15–25-knot northeasterlies during the season.

Type and size of boat: Power or sail, 25ft (7.6m) plus.

Equipment: Charts, chartplotter, depth sounder, anchor, binoculars and bimini.

Tides: Minimal tidal range, between 30–46cm.

Hazards: No major hazards, although approach to Anegada requires some skill, as it is low-lying and surrounded by reefs.

Suitable for night sailing: Yes, although Anegada should not be approached at night.

Difficulty of route: Easy to moderate.

Skills required: Good boat handling, ability to anchor and excellent pilotage skills for approach to Anegada.

Charts: Imray: A23 (Virgin Islands and St Croix), A231 (Virgin Islands), A232 (Virgin Islands). Admiralty: 2006 (West Indies – Virgin Islands; Anegada to St Thomas), 2005 (Road Harbour to Capella Islands), 2019 (North Sound to Road Harbour), 2020 (Harbours and Anchorages in the British Virgin Islands).

Berthing/mooring: Tortola: marinas at Nanny Cay, Parham Town in Fat Hogs Bay, Road Harbour and West End (Soper's Hole); Virgin Gorda: Spanish Town and Bitter End Yacht Club; Peter Island: Sprat Bay. Moorings and anchorages can be found off the other main islands: Norman Island, Anegada, Jost Van Dyke and Cooper Island, and at Cane Garden Bay on the north coast of Tortola.

Ports of entry: Road Harbour and Soper's Hole on Tortola, Great Harbour on Jost Van Dyke, Gun Creek and Spanish Town on Virgin Gorda.

Water: Available at all of the marinas.

Provisioning: Widely available at the larger towns, such as Road Town and Soper's Hole on Tortola and Spanish Town on Virgin Gorda. Modest provisions are available at other destinations.

Fuel: Available at all of the marinas.

Shorepower: Available at all of the marinas.

Maintenance: Full boatyard facilities at most of the marinas.

Family friendliness: Very family friendly.

Further reading: *Grenada to the Virgin Islands* by Jacques Patuelli; *Cruising Guides to the Virgin Islands* by Simon and Nancy Scott; *Street's Guide Puerto Rico, Passage and Virgin Islands* by Don Street; *A Cruising Guide to the Virgin Islands* by Stephen J Pavlidis; *Virgin Islands NV-Cruising Guide* by NV Charts.

left The start and end of this cruise is Tortola, which is a good place to get provisions and find a sheltered anchorage.

VOYAGE 16

Mexico

THE SEA OF CORTEZ

The Sea of Cortez, or Gulf of California, as it is also known, lies between the Baja California peninsula and mainland Mexico. Extending for around 700nm, and with an average breadth of 90nm, it is Mexico's most popular cruising destination, and one that is well-loved by sailors in the northwest Pacific too.

While the northern half of the Sea of Cortez poses potentially tricky conditions, with huge tidal ranges and strong winds, the southern end is much more benign and cruiser-friendly. There is a decent smattering of anchorages, a pleasant climate and sailing conditions to suit most abilities.

Although the southern Sea of Cortez is a popular destination with cruising yachts, it is largely unspoilt and has retained much of its character. In fact, apart from the start and end destinations on this route, there are few facilities, and part of its charm is its remoteness. Much of the route is dominated by a mountain range called the Sierra de la Giganta (Giant Woman), which provides shelter for yachts in coastal waters. Although La Paz and Puerto Escondido are substantial in their extent and facilities, you will encounter few other settlements of any size.

In peak season you may find yourself having to share anchorages with other boats, but the area's rural, rugged beauty more than makes up for it. The snorkelling and diving are good too, as are the prehistoric cave paintings and hot springs to be found along the coast. The biggest treat, however, is when the sun sets and the clouds clear to reveal the most impressive array of stars you will have ever seen.

below The Sea of Cortez, despite its fabulous scenery, remains mostly unspoilt.

above Pelicans stand guard over the shallow, crystal-clear seas that surrond La Paz.

The route

This route is a linear passage that explores the southeast coast of the Baja California peninsula, from La Paz to Puerto Escondido. The cruise starts at the port of La Paz, before heading 7nm to a small cove at Caleta Lobos. From here, it is a 15nm sail to two islands – Isla Espiritu Santo, which lies to the north of La Paz and the neighbouring Isla Partida, which lies immediately off its north coast.

You could easily spend several days here, before making the next 15nm passage to Isla San José, farther north-northwest up the Baja peninsula. The Amortajada Lagoon on the island's southwest coast is the largest mangrove lagoon on the Sea of Cortez and can be explored by dinghy from Bahía Amortajada in settled conditions. Alternatively, Bahía San Evaristo on the peninsula side of the San José Channel provides two well-protected anchorages, in the northeastern and southern corners of the bay.

Following the coastline in a northwesterly direction, your next port of call is Isla Santa Cruz, where you can anchor off the east coast, before arriving at the twin coves of Gato and Toro (which translate as Cat and Bull), 12nm to the northwest on the Baja peninsula. From here it is another short sail to Bahía Agua Verde, 2nm west of Punta San Marcial, before the route continues north to Isla Carmen and the anchorages in Bahía Salinas. The route then concludes by sailing down the south coast of the island before heading between it and Isla Danzante Primero and northwest towards the narrow entrance at Puerto Escondido.

Destinations

La Paz: The start destination of La Paz and its surrounding municipality is Mexico's fourth largest city, with a harbour that caters well for visiting boats. Tucked into a crook of the Sea of Cortez, the city stands on the eastern shore of the Ensenada de La Paz, a large, attractive and near-fully enclosed bay that offers shelter from all directions and in all conditions, even hurricanes. Shallow in places, it offers a good anchorage, although expect to pay for each day you anchor here. Alternatively, there are five marinas to choose from, all within easy reach of the city and with excellent facilities. A useful source of information on cruising this area is the Club Cruceros de La Paz at Marina de La Paz. For provisioning, La Paz is very good too, so make sure you stock up before embarking on the cruise.

Isla Espiritu Santo and Isla Partida: Lying immediately to the north of La Paz, Isla Espiritu Santo is joined to its neighbouring island, Isla Partida, via a thin isthmus of sand. Both islands offer numerous anchorages along their deeply indented shores, and are a UNESCO-recognized Biosphere Reserve, a protected ecosystem that fosters a harmonious and sustainable relationship between the people that use it and the environment.

Amortajada Lagoon: This large mangrove estuary is unlike anywhere else you will encounter on this route. Lush and verdant vegetation dominate in contrast to the barren terrain elsewhere, and although not suitable for deep draught yachts to enter, it is certainly a worthy destination to explore by dinghy. Bahía Amortajada, on which the entrance to the lagoon lies, offers reasonable shelter, but watch out for the sandbars.

Gato and Toro: The twin bays of Gato and Toro lie 2nm to the north of Timbabichi, and offer two places to anchor overnight. Both are picturesque, with distinctive pink and red sandstone cliffs flanking the bay's shores, but should only be considered in settled conditions, as space is minimal.

Bahía Agua Verde: Named after the turquoise waters that line this bay, Bahía Agua Verde is a wide bay that offers three different places to anchor, as well as a tiny village, beaches and caves to explore. The north-west corner offers the best anchorage, although care should be taken to avoid the submerged rock.

Puerto Escondido: The final destination on this route, Puerto Escondido, means 'Hidden Port' in English, and from the sea it can be hard to identify the narrow entrance to the bay. Once inside, however, you will find a fabulous and secure anchorage, which is particularly popular during the hurricane season. It is also home to the Hidden Port Yacht Club, a useful source of information. For provisions, head to Loreto, to the north.

Level of skill

You need to be self-sufficient on this cruise. Although it is not a particularly lengthy route (it could be completed in seven days) the only real facilities available are at the start and end destinations of La Paz and Puerto Escondido. The rest of the cruise comprises anchorages, mostly in remote areas. The villages that you will pass en route are small and have relatively few facilities, so it is important that you stock up well ahead with food, water and fuel. La Paz and Puerto Escondido are major boating centres, so all of your needs and requirements should be met there.

Similarly, because the marinas and moorings are confined to the start and finish of the route, it is crucial that you have good anchoring skills. There are at least 12 anchorages to choose from between Isla Espiritu Santo and Puerto Escondido, but they vary in size and popularity. Either end of the season you may get an anchorage to yourself, but in peak season it is highly unlikely, so an ability to anchor in close proximity with other boats is essential.

Generally, the anchorages offer good holding, with sandy bottoms and about 6–8m of water. Check the wind direction before anchoring, and if in doubt as to whether a bay is tenable, consider moving elsewhere. Most of the anchorages are within easy reach of each other, and if one isn't suitable, another may be.

The prevailing wind in this part of the Sea of Cortez is from the northwest, and during the main sailing season is usually fairly benign. Watch out for Northers, though. These are very strong northerly winds that blow down the length of the Sea of Cortez from the USA, and can be particularly unpleasant to be caught out in, as

above Sailing conditions are great but watch out for the short squally storms that can affect this coast.

winds can often exceed 40 knots, with subsequent swell and chop. If there is any sign of a Norther coming in, find a sheltered anchorage fast. Chubascos, or short squally storms, can also be a problem during the summer months.

When to go

It is possible to sail year-round in the Sea of Cortez, although the very real threat of the hurricane season between 1 June and 31 October means that in fact most people head to this region between early November and late May. Should you find yourself there during the hurricane season, the start and end destinations of La Paz and Puerto Escondido do offer hurricane holes, but the scorching temperatures experienced here during the peak summer months may deter you as they can reach in excess of 38°C (100°F).

Between November and May temperatures are mild but still very pleasant, with average highs of 24–30°C (75–86°F). Sunshine is pretty much guaranteed all year, and this region only receives about 15cm (6in) rain annually. During the winter months temperatures at night can drop considerably, but after the heat of the day this is not unbearable.

Ideally, autumn and spring are the best times to visit, as then the temperatures are comfortable and the water deliciously warm, but the numbers of cruising boats are still low enough to mean that you may get some anchorages to yourself.

THE SEA OF CORTEZ AT A GLANCE

Route length: Around 140nm.

Time required: Two to three weeks.

When to go: Year-round, but to avoid the hurricane season visit between November and May.

Weather: Tropical climate with mild winters and hot summers. Average highs during the sailing season are between 24 and 30°C (75 and 86°F).

Type and size of boat: Power or sail, 25ft (7.6m) plus.

Equipment: Charts, chartplotter, depth sounder, safety equipment, VHF radio, compass, GPS, anchors, EPIRB, bimini, dinghy.

Tides: A tidal range of about 1.5m in the southern Sea of Cortez, but significantly bigger tides of around 9m to the north.

Hazards: Rocks, squally conditions.

Suitable for night sailing: No.

Difficulty of route: Moderate to difficult.

Skills required: Ability to be self-sufficient and to anchor within close proximity of other boats.

Charts: Imray: 1017 (Golfo de California), 3061 (Plans in the Golfo de California). The Mexican Navy also produce good charts.

Berthing/mooring: Good choice of marinas at La Paz and one at Puerto Escondido, but only anchorages in the area in between.

Port of entry: La Paz.

Water: Available at the marinas in La Paz and Puerto Escondido only.

Provisioning: Make sure you stock up with provisions prior to leaving La Paz as there are no other opportunities on the route. Limited supplies are available at Puerto Escondido, but a good selection of supplies at Loreto to the north.

Fuel: Available at the marinas in La Paz and Puerto Escondido only.

Shorepower: Available at the marinas in La Paz and Puerto Escondido only.

Maintenance: Full-service marinas and boatyard facilities at La Paz and some services at marina at Puerto Escondido. There are no other services on the route.

Family friendliness: This area is remote, so although La Paz is home to many attractions to entertain children, the rest of the route offers few commercial activities/days out. If, however, you as a family enjoy beachcombing, snorkelling, diving and discovering wildlife, then this area has much to offer.

Further reading: *Sea of Cortez, a Cruiser's Guidebook* by Shawn Breeding; *Mexico Boating Guide* by Patricia Rains.

VOYAGE 17

United States

THE SAN JUAN ISLANDS

Anyone with an interest in marine mammals should explore the San Juan Islands. This archipelago, which lies off the USA's northwest coast, 60nm north of Seattle and close to the border with Canada, is home to several pods of orcas, and is regularly visited by transient pods. River otters, minke whales, seals and Steller sea lions have made this area their home too. Ashore you'll find continental USA's largest concentration of bald eagles, soaring above the pine forests that cover much of the archipelago's landscape.

As a destination for wildlife lovers, the San Juan Islands rate highly, and there are plenty of opportunities to witness it. There are over 400 islands and islets within the archipelago, only around half of which are named, offering over 725km (450 miles) of shoreline to explore, as well as many anchorages and marinas.

The sailing here is excellent too with the long protective arm of Vancouver Island sheltering the archipelago from the worst of the weather. Once you get used to the strong tidal currents, there is much to suit all abilities. Distances between the islands are generally short, but if you want to explore farther afield you can, with Puget Sound and Seattle lying to the south, and Vancouver to the north.

The archipelago was first discovered and charted by European explorers in 1791, when the Spaniard Francisco de Eliza came across them during an expedition. He named the islands San Juan after the Viceroy of Mexico, under whose authority he sailed. Today it is a popular tourist destination, and one of the USA's finest locations.

below The start point of this cruise is Bellingham Bay, set in a breathtaking landscape.

The route

This route is an anticlockwise circumnavigation of the San Juan Islands, which visits some of the archipelago's most attractive islands, including Cypress Island, Orcas Islands, San Juan Island and Lopez Island. In total, the route is about 160nm, which can be covered in about a fortnight at a reasonably leisurely pace.

The start destination on this route is Squalicum Harbor at Bellingham, in the northeast corner of Bellingham Bay. From here, head southwest across Bellingham Bay to Inati Bay on the southeast corner of Lummi Island. You can then either spend the night here, or after a lunchtime stop continue southwest to Pelican Beach on Cypress Island.

From Pelican Beach, head north round the easternmost tip of Orcas Island and then northwest to Clark, before continuing northwest to Matia, one of the Boundary Islands. It is then another short hop to Sucia,

another of the Boundary Islands, which lies to the northwest, before the route heads southwest to Stuart Island. From here, head east to the west coast of Orcas Island and Deer Harbor, or continue eastwards until you reach the large channel that nearly cuts the island in half. East Sound offers numerous anchoring possibilities.

From here, head southwest between Shaw Island to Lopez Island, before turning northwest to run up the northeast coast of San Juan Island. The route then continues around the coast of San Juan Island, via Roche Harbor on the northwest corner, and around the south coast of Lopez Island, before heading to Anacortes on Fidalgo and then back to Inati Bay and Bellingham.

below San Juan Island offers the best place to watch the remarkable acrobatics of the resident orca population.

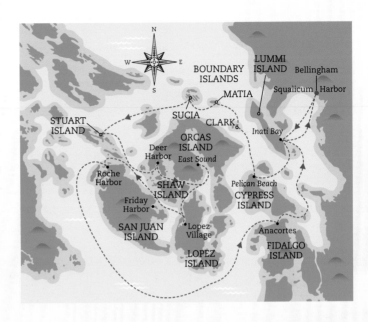

Destinations

Cypress Island: If you are looking for good walks ashore, then Cypress Island is one to explore. The trails here, particularly the Eagle Cliff Trail, at the northern end of the island, which leads from one of the island's anchorages, Pelican Beach, is particularly good, and you are guaranteed to see stunning views of the archipelago and a cornucopia of wildlife. The anchorage at Eagle Harbor, to the south-southeast of Pelican Beach is also good, although it can get busy peak season.

Boundary Islands: This mini archipelago lies to the north of Orcas Island and is the northernmost group within the San Juan Islands. It comprises Patos Island, Sucia Island and Matia Island, as well as numerous rocks and islets. The middle island, Sucia, has over 50 mooring buoys and several cable moorings and floating pontoons available for hire. Echo Bay, on the middle of the east coast, is the largest anchorage, with good holding on mud. There are also mooring buoys here, but beware the marked eel grass beds as no anchoring is permitted there. Alternatively, Ewing Cove to the west of Ewing Island on the northeastern tip of Sucia Island, is a stunning place to drop your hook, as is Fossil Bay to the south.

Stuart Island: Both the north and south coastlines of Stuart Island provide a number of places to anchor and spend the day or night, and most of which offer good all-round protection in most conditions. Part of the island is now a marine park, and this maintains around 12 visitors' moorings in Reid Harbor and a further 10 in Prevost Harbor on the north coast. There are also pontoon berths available, although space is at a premium. The Turn Point Light Station is also an interesting place to visit if you fancy a wander.

Orcas Island: Orcas Island lies to the north of Lopez Island and is shaped like a horseshoe. It is the hilliest of the islands, with the tallest peak, Mount Constitution, rising to 734m (2,408ft). A trek up the wooded mountain is well recommended, if only to see the stunning views and the Mountain Lake located in the middle of the eastern arm of the island. Anchorages and moorings can be found at Deer Harbor and East Sound, and there are several marinas open to visiting yachts.

Lopez Island: One of the three main islands, Lopez Island lies in the central southern part of the group. It is the least hilly of the main islands, with gentle undulating terrain dominating much of it. Lopez Village lies on the west of the island and is well supplied. Here, much of the island's fishing history is recorded at the fascinating Lopez Island Historical Society and Museum.

San Juan Island: If it is the orcas that you are hoping to see during your cruise of the archipelago, then head off to the west coast of San Juan Island. Here, at Lime Kiln Point State Park, you can watch the three pods of resident orcas, which can number up to 80 individuals. Friday Harbor, on the northeast coast, is the island group's main port of entry, while there is a seasonal customs office at Roche Harbor on the northwest tip of the island.

Level of skill

As with all island sailing, rocks are the biggest hazard within the San Juan Islands group. There are over 400 islands within this archipelago; some are big and obvious, others are not, so it is crucial that you continually consult your charts and keep a good lookout, as well as paying attention to the state of the tide. Some rocks are submerged at High Water, although without sufficient clearance to allow safe passage over them. In particular, watch out for the submerged rocks to the west of Reid Harbor, off the southeast tip of Stuart Island. The Wasp Passage near Yellow Island, to the southwest of Deer Harbor on Orcas Island, is another troublesome area, as is the narrow Pole Pass, a 12.2m (40ft) wide channel near Bell Island and Mosquito Pass, which runs to the south of Roche Harbor on San Juan Island and to the delightfully sheltered anchorages of Garrison Bay and Westcott Bay.

Although the tidal range of 1.8–3.7m is not unusual, the tidal currents that often flow through this area can be very tricky. Particular care should be taken when transiting narrow channels between the islands as the current is often fast-moving and turbulent. If in doubt, stick to the main wider routes, and avoid areas such as the Mosquito Pass and Pole Pass. The entrance to Fisherman Bay on the west coast of Lopez Island can also be difficult.

Despite this the San Juan islands, along with Puget Sound, form part of the Salish Sea, and conditions here are generally settled – the long, protective arm of Vancouver Island sheltering the waters from the worst of the Pacific Northwest weather. Conditions can deteriorate, but there are enough destinations that it is relatively easy to find somewhere to shelter. Watch out for localized squally and changeable conditions, however, caused by the topography of some of the islands. East Sound on Orcas Island can be susceptible to strong winds if northerlies are blowing.

When to go

The San Juan Islands enjoy a relatively long sailing season, which runs from April to October. Of these months, July and August are generally the warmest, averaging temperatures of 21–27°C (70–81°F). The sailing then is very pleasant, although expect this part of the season to be busy with other visitors to the archipelago. Spring and autumn are a good time to visit, as temperatures are still good, and the waters are less busy with tourists, although fog can be a problem in late summer and early autumn.

Situated so close to the Olympic Mountains, you would expect the San Juan Islands to experience significant rainfall. However, the islands enjoy their own microclimate, lying within the mountain's rain shadow, which means that only around 46cm (18in) falls annually. November, December and January are the wettest months, and the coldest too, with temperatures averaging 3–6°C (37–43°F).

THE SAN JUAN ISLANDS AT A GLANCE

Route length: Around 160nm.

Time required: At least two weeks.

When to go: April to October.

Weather: Summer temperatures average 21–27°C (70–81°F), but November, December and January are considerably colder and wet. Snow that settles is unusual, but fog is a regular occurrence in late summer and early autumn.

Type and size of boat: Power or sail, 25ft (7.6m) plus.

Equipment: Charts, chartplotter, depth sounder.

Tides: Tidal range is 1.8–3.7m; currents are strong in places owing to narrow channels between the islands and an uneven seabed.

Hazards: Rocks, strong currents, other boats.

Suitable for night sailing: No.

Difficulty of route: Moderate.

Skills required: Good navigation and pilotage and the ability to anchor and pick up a mooring.

Charts: NOAA charts: 18400 (Strait of Georgia and Strait of Juan de Fuca), 18421 (Strait of Juan de Fuca to Strait of Georgia; Drayton Harbor), 18423 (Folio Small-Craft – Bellingham to Everett Including San Juan Islands), 18424 (Bellingham Bay; Bellingham Harbor), 18427 (Anacortes to Skagit Bay), 18431 (Rosario Strait to Cherry Point), 18432 (Boundary Pass), 18433 (Haro-Strait-Middle Bank to Stuart Island), 18434 (San Juan Channel).

Berthing/mooring: A wide choice of marinas throughout the archipelago on San Juan Island, Orcas Island, Lopez Island, Fidalgo Island and on the mainland at Bellingham Bay. Numerous anchorages and mooring buoys in bays around the islands.

Ports of entry: Friday Harbor and Roche Harbor on San Juan Island, although the latter is seasonal only. Other ports of entry are at Anacortes as well as Bellingham.

Water: Widely available at marinas throughout the archipelago.

Provisioning: Good range of shops at the mainland and island destinations. Most supplies are within easy reach.

Fuel: Available from most marinas within the San Juan Islands, or at Bellingham.

Shorepower: Widely available at marinas throughout the archipelago.

Maintenance: Range of boatyard services available at the marinas.

Family friendliness: Very. Fantastic wildlife to interest all the family. Numerous beaches and sites ashore.

Further reading: *A Cruising Guide to Puget Sound and the San Juan Islands: Olympia to Port Angeles* by Migael Scherer; *Dreamspeaker Volume 4 – The San Juan Islands* by Anne and Laurence Yeadon-Jones.

left Orcas Island is the most mountainous island so it's the perfect place to get an amazing view of the whole area.

VOYAGE 18
United States

THE INTRACOASTAL WATERWAY

If you are looking to explore the east coast of America but don't fancy experiencing the hazards of sailing up the exposed Atlantic coast, then it may be worth considering the Intracoastal Waterway (ICW). Not only is it a navigable route that offers good shelter and facilities, but it is also a fascinating place to explore in its own right.

The 2,600nm waterway is divided into three unconnected sections: the Atlantic Intracoastal Waterway, which extends from Norfolk, Virginia, to Miami in Florida; and two parts of the Gulf Intracoastal Waterway, which runs from Brownsville, Texas, to Fort Myers in Florida, excluding a section between Carrabelle and Tarpon Springs that has never been joined together.

Initial plans for the ICW, as a means of improving commercial transportation along the Eastern Seaboard, were originally mooted in the late 1700s, but it wasn't until the late 19th and early 20th centuries that the plans came to fruition. Today, commercial craft still use the waterway, although it is leisure craft that are its biggest users and several thousand now ply its waters each year.

The main part of the ICW – the Atlantic ICW – passes through some of America's most historically significant sites and towns. With plenty of marinas and anchorages along its length, there is ample opportunity to stop off and explore. It is also a fascinating place to encounter an impressive and diverse range of wildlife, while transiting a range of waterways to suit all abilities and interests.

below The Intracoastal Waterway, shown here at Pompano Beach, Florida, is a great alternative to the more challenging Atlantic coast.

above Despite its name, the Great Dismal Swamp, which flanks the canal of the same name, is a magical place.

The route

It is not possible to travel the whole length of the ICW in one go, owing to two breaks along the route. However, of the three sections, it is the route from Norfolk in Virginia to Miami in Florida that is the most popular with cruisers, and is the section that this route concentrates on.

The section from Virginia to Miami is fairly self-explanatory. Owing to the number of marinas and destinations along the way, there is no set itinerary – where you stop and how often depends on your own preference and the speed at which you are travelling. However, there is one small diversion that is heartily recommended. Not far from Norfolk, you can access the wonderfully named Great Dismal Swamp Canal, which contrary to its name is a natural gem. This canal can then be followed to the Pasquotank River, before entering the Albermarle Sound and rejoining the main route.

From here the route continues south, skirting to the west of Pamlico Sound, via Beaufort/Morehead City, Wilmington, Georgetown, Charleston, Brunswick, Daytona Beach, Fort Pierce and Fort Lauderdale, before arriving at Miami.

Charts are the most essential piece of equipment to have on board when transiting the ICW, although the route is generally well marked with aids to navigation. These are principally daymarks on piles or dolphins, and a number of buoys too. All aids to navigation have a reflective yellow square or triangle symbol on them, and the symbols should be followed according to which direction you are travelling in. For example, all triangles indicate aids should be passed on the starboard side of the vessel while the squares indicate aids should be kept to port, but they are reversed when heading in the other direction.

Destinations

Norfolk: The starting destination of this route is at the southern end of Norfolk Bay and the mouth of Chesapeake Bay. Founded in 1682, Norfolk now has a population of over 250,000 and is a busy naval and commercial port. Sites to see include the Chrysler Museum of Art, Fort Norfolk, Norfolk State University Planetarium and Norfolk Botanical Garden.

Great Dismal Swamp Canal: This canal runs along the eastern edge of the Great Dismal Swamp and dates to 1793 when digging work started. It is the oldest man-made canal in the USA and has been in continuous use since 1805. As well as being essential for the transportation of goods, it was also strategically important for both opposing sides during the American Civil War (1861–65). Today, it is used by over 2,000 boats every year, and the Great Dismal Swamp National Wildlife Refuge and Lake Drummond, which it flanks, is a fascinating place to explore. Tree-lined and densely vegetated, the Great Dismal Swamp Canal is a quiet and interesting alternative to the main route.

Albermarle Sound: This large estuary has a fearsome reputation among mariners, but on a calm day can be a placid piece of water to cross. Situated about 56nm south of Norfolk, it is protected from the Atlantic by the Outer Banks, but its shallow water can produce interesting conditions should the wind deteriorate. Once home to the native Algonquian Indians, who used dugout canoes to travel its waters, the shores around the estuary were first colonized by European explorers in 1586. Fishing for shad and herring was a major industry here too, but overfishing in the 21st century has led to a significant decline in the numbers of fish.

Georgetown: This area is thought to be the first place to be colonized in North America, when the Europeans settled here in 1526. The town, around 660km (410 miles) south of Norfolk is today home to over 10,000 people and it is a delightful place to stop. It is dominated by one of the world's largest paper mills, which has been in operation since 1937, as well as a steel mill, but you'll also find several marinas and anchorages close to the town's waterfront and a number of attractions to visit.

Charleston: Continue on the ICW for around 45nm to the town of Charleston, which forms the divide between the Cooper and Ashley rivers. It's the oldest city in South Carolina and one filled with interesting architecture, historical sites and culture. The 17-day Spoleto Festival USA (May/June) is worth visiting for its theatre, music and dance events, as are its museums.

Miami: This city is a complete contrast to Charleston. Known as the 'capital of Latin America' it is also one of the richest cities in the USA and an extremely busy port for cruise ships. It's not to everyone's taste maybe, but facilities are good, and it is also the gateway to the Florida Keys, providing a whole new area of coastal cruising to be explored.

left Charleston is well worth exploring for its numerous cultural events, museums and historical sites.

Level of skill

Transiting this 940nm-stretch of waterway does require a certain amount of skill and experience. The ICW is formed of canals, rivers, bays, wide estuaries and narrow creeks, all of which bring their own areas of trickiness. It is generally well protected from the worst Atlantic weather, but at times it can still be exposed to it. During the summer months winds tend to be light, but can be stronger at other times of the year. This can produce choppy conditions, particularly where the ICW runs close to the coast and if the current is travelling in the opposite direction.

For most people, negotiating these sort of conditions is no more difficult than offshore sailing, although the proximity of the shoreline and the number of leisure craft in the area can make it more tricky. In fact, it is the other leisure craft using the ICW that are the biggest hazard. During the summer months the ICW can get very busy, so it is crucial that you know and adhere to the Rules of the Road. Commercial craft also use the waterway but are usually very considerate to boatowners. If you are unsure of a vessel's intentions or wish to overtake them, then it is important to contact them on VHF Channel 13, as most commercial craft monitor this frequency.

Other hazards to be aware of include the tides, which affect certain stretches of the ICW. Some of the ICW is non-tidal, but other parts, and particularly where there are inlets from it to the sea, are tidal. Tidal ranges vary, but are usually 1–2.4m, with bigger tides (2.4–6.7m) affecting the southern part of the route. Currents can run at up to 3 knots, and are particularly noticeable in narrower stretches, or under bridges, where the waterway is constricted. You will also find yourself affected by incoming currents at the coastal inlets, which may set you sideways out of the channel. Boats moving with the current have right of way at all times.

And finally on this 940nm-route from Norfolk to Miami, you will encounter over 140 bridges. Many of these are high enough, with an air draught of 19.8m, so they will not pose much of a problem. However, just over half of the bridges are too low for transiting, which means that they will have to be opened to let you through. Some will open specifically for you, but for others you will have to time your approach as they operate a timetable of openings.

When to go

The advantage of sailing the east coast via the Intracoastal Waterway is that it is suitable for transit at all times of the year. The protected waters offer reasonable shelter from the strong Atlantic winds and with a wealth of destinations along the route, there are plenty of places to duck into should conditions deteriorate. Generally, however, the best time to transit the waterway is either in the spring or autumn, although these can also be the busiest months and fog can be a problem too.

The climate in this part of the USA is within the humid subtropical zone, which sees hot and humid summers and mild winters. Temperatures during the summer months range from 18°C to 32°C (64°F to 90°F), and winds are often very light, while during the winter temperatures average 14–28°C (57–82°F). During the spring and autumn months, the nights are generally cool, while the days are warm.

THE INTRACOASTAL WATERWAY AT A GLANCE

Route length: 940nm.

Time required: At least 4 weeks, but may be longer depending on the size and speed of your boat and how often you stop off.

When to go: It can be transited year-round, but the best seasons are spring and autumn.

Weather: Hot humid summers and mild winters, with light winds during the summer months. Annual temperatures range from 14°C to 32°C (57°F to 90°F).

Type and size of boat: Power or sail, 25ft (7.6m) plus. It is possible to sail some stretches of the ICW, but most of it requires you to be under power, so a boat with a decent engine is essential. Deeper-draught boats may struggle with parts of the ICW too. Depths vary from 1.8–3.7m, but dredging is sporadic, and boats drawing 1.8m may run aground at times.

Equipment: Charts, tide and current tables, VHF radio, anchor, mooring lines, depth sounder, fog horn.

Tides: The ICW is a mixture of tidal and non-tidal waters. The tidal range in some places, such as Georgia, is 2.4–6.7m. Tidal currents vary, but can be up to 3 knots. There are strong currents in narrow channels.

Hazards: Other boats, strong currents, debris in the water, tides, bridges.

Suitable for night sailing: No, although it is possible with care.

Difficulty of route: Moderate to hard.

Skills required: Ability to manoeuvre a boat under power in close quarters and good anchoring skills.

Charts: NOAA small-craft charts, *Intracoastal Waterway Chartbook*.

Berthing/mooring: On average, there are marinas every 20nm or so. Berthing is generally alongside. There are numerous anchorages en route.

Ports of entry: Norfolk, Miami.

Water: Widely available at various marinas along the route.

Provisioning: Widely available from towns and marinas along the route.

Fuel: Available from marinas along the route.

Shorepower: Most marinas along the route can provide shorepower.

Maintenance: A range of boatyard facilities, including repair, mechanical engineering and general maintenance, can be found either at marinas or in towns along the route.

Family friendliness: Very family friendly as there are lots of places to stop off en route.

Further reading: *The Intracoastal Waterway* by Jan and Bill Moeller; *The Intracoastal Waterway Chartbook* (International Marine).

VOYAGE 19

Canada

LAKE HURON

Cruising on inland waterways can be an idyllic way to spend a sailing holiday – as we have seen in the French canals and the Intracoastal Waterway in the USA. However, the pinnacle, and most extreme of inland waterways is Canada's Great Lakes – vast expanses that account for a fifth of the world's supply of fresh water, and a destination you could spend years exploring, such is its scale.

In total, the five interconnected Great Lakes cover 244,000sq km (94,000 square miles). Of the lakes, Lake Huron is the most central and the second largest at 332km (206 miles) long and 295km (183 miles) wide.

The cruising potential of Lake Huron is huge, and a circuit of the lake could be completed within a month. However, in the northern half of the lake lies one of its main delights – the North Channel and Georgian Bay. This area is incredible for its rugged natural beauty, relatively unspoiled in terms of urbanization, and is a fascinating cruising ground to explore.

Do not be fooled by the word 'lake' when considering the level of skill required to sail Lake Huron. This is an area known for its extreme weather conditions and it can be a treacherous place for the uninitiated. That said, the quieter, more protected stretches of the North Channel are an idyllic place for what is known as 'gunkholing'. A gunkhole refers to a shallow, muddy place – and there are plenty of these locations to meander through, staying overnight in bays and coves and on the islands.

below Killarney is a lovely, quiet location for starting your exploration of the North Channel.

The route

With 6,159km (3,827 miles) of coastline, there are plenty of places to start a cruise of Lake Huron from. Many people choose to start from Sarnia in the southernmost part of Lake Huron. However, there are many boats passing through this port between Lake St Claire and Lake Erie, making it very busy with ships and commercial traffic. A popular alternative lies on the north coast of Lake Huron at Killarney. From here you can explore the delights of the North Channel in more protected waters.

This route is a clockwise circumnavigation of the North Channel, but it can be extended further by heading east into Georgian Bay or south into Lake Huron itself. From Killarney, head 4nm to the charming anchorage of Covered Portage, which lies to the northeast of Sheep Island. The route then continues southwest for around 20nm through the channel to the north of Badgeley, Centre and Partridge islands to Little Current on Manitoulin Island. A swing bridge spans the gap between Manitoulin Island and Goat

Island at Little Current, but opens for passing boat traffic every 15 minutes.

From Little Current, continue northeast to Croker Island and the Benjamin Islands, 17nm away, before heading east to Meldrum Bay on Manitoulin Island, and then a farther 50nm to DeTour village, which lies on the mainland, a short distance off the western end of Drummond Island. Anyone wishing to extend the cruise then has the option of continuing northwest to Lake Superior or south to the main part of Lake Huron.

Continuing on the main route, head northeast from DeTour village to Thessalon for around 20nm, before sailing east to the Whalesback Channel and Bear Drop Harbor. You then have numerous options of destinations along the return journey back to Killarney, including the stunning Baie Fine, the entrance of which lies 12nm northeast of Little Current. From here, sail east again via Partridge, Centre and Badgeley Islands back to Killarney.

Destinations

Killarney: The start and end destination of this cruise is a popular stopover with visiting yachts. Situated on the north coast of Lake Huron, at the eastern end of the North Channel, Killarney is home to six marinas and excellent facilities. The town itself dates to 1820, and now forms part of the Killarney Provincial Park, a wilderness preserve that is home to a diverse ecosystem. The scenery around here, which includes areas of dense pine forests, crystal-clear waters and the soaring peaks of La Cloche Mountains, is stunning and well worth exploring.

Covered Portage: This unusually named anchorage lies just 4nm northeast of Killarney and is a gem of a destination. To enter the cove you have to go through a narrow entrance channel, but once inside you will find a perfectly sheltered hideaway, protected by steep-sided rocky cliffs. It's a popular spot with cruising boats, and often quiet at either end of the season.

Manitoulin Island: Well known as the world's largest island on a freshwater lake, Manitoulin Island covers 2,849sq km (1,100 square miles) and forms the southern coast of the North Channel. Protecting the 160nm waterway from the ravages of the rest of Lake Huron, its southern shores are relatively inhospitable, and as a result, it rarely attracts visiting yachts. Its north coast, in contrast, is pitted with bays and coves offering a huge range of alternative places to anchor. Villages and small towns can also be found here, including Little Current, on the eastern tip of the island, which is linked to Goat Island via a swing bridge across the narrowest part of the North Channel. Little Current is the biggest town on the island and here you will be able to find a good range of facilities, including a marina.

Benjamin Islands: This group of islands is situated 17nm west of Little Current. Formed of pink granite, the island group comprises two main islands, North Benjamin and South Benjamin, which are surrounded by a collection of smaller islets. The two anchorages of note lie to the south of South Benjamin, and are identifiable by the distinctive 'Sow and Pigs' islets that mark the approach.

Baie Fine: The fjord-like Baie Fine looks distinctly Scandinavian in origin on first approach. Lying 12nm northeast of Little Current on Manitoulin Island, it is one of the world's largest freshwater fjords and a stunning destination for anyone exploring the North Channel, with plenty of places to anchor. Follow the 9nm-long channel through pine-fringed, white-rock cliffs and you will eventually reach the Pool. This is another delightful anchorage, although it is often quite full of weeds.

Level of skill

Lake Huron can be a tricky place to sail for the unwary, its reputation marred by countless tales of shipwrecks and disasters, most notably the Great Storm of 1913. The vast expanse of Lake Huron allows swell a long distance to build up, and combined with strong winds can make for tricky conditions for the inexperienced and experienced sailor alike. Careful consideration of the weather before setting out is therefore essential, although it can be hard to prepare for the powerful thunderstorms that can blow up relatively quickly here.

This route around the North Channel benefits from the protection of the north coast of Manitoulin Island, which shields it from the worst of Lake Huron's weather. However, heavy swell can still build up here, fetching from east to west, so avoid sailing upwind if conditions deteriorate. The route offers plenty of sheltered anchorages, however, and because the bays and islands are so numerous, if one isn't suitable, another close by surely will be.

Another hazard is the geography of the islands themselves. This area is not recommended for night sailing as it is heavily strewn with rocks, islets and islands, many of which are unmarked. This means it is essential that you maintain a good lookout at all times. Some of the channels between the islands are also narrow. For example, the Whaleback Channel, on which Bear Drop Harbor stands, measures just 50m (164ft) wide in places.

The majority of the anchorages offer secure holding on sand or mud, but many boatowners choose to run a line from the stern or bow ashore for added protection. Depths vary considerably, often within a short distance, so keep an eye on your depth sounder.

Although this area does require quite a bit of experience to explore comfortably, it is such a stunning area in terms of rugged, natural beauty, that the trickiness of the sailing makes the final destination that bit more rewarding.

When to go

The sailing season on Lake Huron is relatively short, running from June to September. During these months temperatures average 13–17°C (55–63°F), with July being the hottest month. August is the busiest month in terms of numbers of boats on the water, so September is a good time to visit. The area is quieter, but the weather is still good, the water is warm and there are fewer mosquitoes around!

The prevailing winds come from a westerly quadrant, with northwesterlies dominating the first half of the season and southwesterlies the latter half. Average wind speeds are 8–15 knots, although in more exposed areas, and certainly in the main body of Lake Huron, they can reach higher figures. Indeed the highest wind speeds since records began were measured in August 1965, when the lake saw 95-knot winds, and in 1996 a subtropical cyclone formed on the lake!

Expect occasional squally conditions during the summer months, with sharp gusts accompanying heavy thunderstorms. These can often build up quickly, covering a large area of the lake, and they are particularly prevalent between June and August. At the start of the season early morning fog can be a regular occurrence too.

LAKE HURON AT A GLANCE

Route length: Around 230nm.

Time required: Two to three weeks, more if possible as the choice of destinations is huge.

When to go: The season runs from June to September, although the busiest month is August. This is when you'll experience the best conditions, and in September, too, although there are usually fewer boats on the water then.

Weather: The weather can be changeable, even during the sailing season. Temperatures average 13–17°C (55–63°F), and July is usually the hottest month. Look out for squalls and sudden thunderstorms at any time, although the North Channel is well protected from the ferocious winds that often dominate Lake Huron itself. Fog can be a problem during the early mornings at the start of the season.

Type and size of boat: Power or sail, 25ft (7.6m) plus.

Equipment: Charts, depth sounder, good anchor, dinghy, reliable engine and outboard for a dinghy.

Tides: No tides to speak of, although changes in pressure can affect water levels very slightly.

Hazards: Unmarked rocks and islets, rapid change of depth within short distance, poor weather conditions, which can generate heavy swell and shipping within the main body of Lake Huron. All shipping movements are governed by the Canadian Coast Guard VTS.

Suitable for night sailing: No. This area is strewn with unmarked rocks, and changes in depths within the channels often occur within just a short distance.

Difficulty of route: Moderate to hard.

Skills required: Thorough knowledge of navigation and interpreting weather forecasts, plus experience of sailing in heavy weather and the ability to anchor.

Charts: Admiralty: 4794 (Canada General Chart, Great Lakes). NOAA chart: 14860 (Lake Huron).

Berthing/mooring: Marinas at Killarney, Little Current, Meldrum Bay, DeTour village and Thessalon. Berthing is a mixture of alongside, stern- and bow-to. Numerous anchorages can be found in the North Channel.

Ports of entry: Blind River and Tobermory.

Water: Widely available at marinas and harbours.

Provisioning: Good choice of places to provision. Most provisions can be found at the larger destinations, while some of the smaller destinations have at least one shop, or are within close reach of a larger harbour.

Fuel: Widely available from the marinas.

Shorepower: Available at the marinas.

Maintenance: This area is well set up for boats and most of the marinas along this route can provide boatyard facilities either on site or nearby.

Family friendliness: This route is very family friendly, with most of the destinations being short hops away from each other. There are creeks and islands aplenty to explore, interesting walks and the bigger towns offer enough commercialised sites of interest to keep younger crew entertained.

Further reading: Nothing up to date is currently available, but have a look online or in second-hand bookshops or marketplaces for used books.

VOYAGE 20
Thailand

PHUKET AND PHANG NGA BAY

Time slows down in Thailand. The pace of life is very relaxed here, and once immersed in the country's stunning landscape, it's not hard to relax and unwind. This cruising area is arguably the best destination in South-East Asia, and a Mecca for many yachts sailing a world circuit.

The choice of destinations to stop at and visit during the day or overnight is huge, with over 1,609km (1,000 miles) of coastline around the mainland to explore, although the route outlined below involves just a tiny percentage of this. The myriad islands that lie within this area provide numerous choices to suit most people and most requirements.

Inevitably, the stunning location and relatively easy sailing conditions make this a particularly popular place to sail, and improved facilities in recent years have done much to establish Thailand on the cruising sailors' map. It is particularly popular with charter boats, with many companies choosing to base themselves at Phuket on Phuket Island; however, this should not deter you from exploring these waters.

This part of Thailand really is a stunning place to explore. Most of the destinations are within easy reach, and the landscape you will discover here is incredible. The crystal-clear, turquoise waters are home to a fascinating underwater paradise to delight divers and snorkellers alike, while the dramatic vertiginous limestone outcrops that erupt out of the sea make a wonderful backdrop. With a climate that is suitable for year-round cruising, a rich cultural heritage and hugely friendly locals, it may be hard to tear yourself away.

below Dramatic limestone outcrops and crystal-clear turquoise seas make Thailand a must-see destination.

The route

The choice of places to cruise in Thailand is vast, but this route takes in some of the most dramatic parts of the country in an area well known for its sheltered sailing and stunning anchorages. It is a relatively short route, although to extend it further you could head up the west coast of Phuket to explore the islands and coastline of the Andaman Sea, including the Similan Islands, a national park since 1982, which lie 65nm northwest of Phuket Island.

The route detailed below, however, is a circular route that explores Phang Nga Bay, a 400-sq km (154-square mile) bay that lies between the east coast of Phuket Island and the Malay Peninsula and its many islands. Aside from the main city of Phuket on Phuket Island and Krabi on the mainland, 55nm to the east, there are no other marina facilities within this route. However, most of the islands offer opportunities to provision or eat out.

above The Koh Phi Phi islands were used as the location for the film The Beach.

The starting destination is Phuket, a city that stands on the east coast of Phuket Island, and is home to four marinas. From here, head south for 29nm to Koh Racha Yai which lies to the south of Phuket Island. It is then a 27nm hop east to the Koh Phi Phi islands, before the route continues 28nm southeast to Koh Lanta off the mainland coast. From there it is a 12nm sail southeast to Koh Muk, before the route heads west to Koh Rok Noi.

It is then another 16nm northwest to Koh Ha Yai, before a 20nm leg north for a second stopover at the Koh Phi Phi islands. From here, head 20nm northeast to Krabi on the mainland and Rai Le Beach, before circumnavigating Phang Nga Bay anticlockwise in a 40nm leg back to Phuket, via the islands of Koh Hong and Koh Khao Phing Kan.

Destinations

Phuket: Thailand's largest island, Phuket is also its yachting centre. Home to four marinas and a steadily increasing number of facilities catering specifically for boat users, the town that bears the same name is a delightful place to explore. All foreign boats arriving in the area must call in at Ao Chalong to complete their paperwork, although much of it can now be completed online in advance. On the island, sites to see include the temple of Wat Phra Thong, which is built around a gold-leafed, half-submerged Buddha; the Phuket Butterfly Garden and Insect World; and the Phuket Marine Biological Center, situated on the southeastern tip of the island. There are also a number of interesting temples within the town itself.

Koh Phi Phi Ley: This island is also well known to film buffs as the location of the adaptation of the Alex Garland novel *The Beach*. Maya Beach, where the film was shot, is an idyllic spot, marred only by the numerous daytrippers that descend on it during the day. Overnight anchoring off the island is only permitted between November and April as Koh Phi Phi Ley is also home to a highly prized bird called the edible-nest swiftlet. The nests of these birds are used for bird's nest soup, and between February and April the caves where the birds make their nests are heavily guarded to prevent poachers. Koh Phi Phi Don, the larger inhabited sister island to Koh Phi Phi Ley lies to the north and is also worth visiting.

Koh Muk: It is the emerald cave on Koh Muk's west coast that is this island's main attraction. If you swim through a long tunnel under the rocks you will eventually reach a stunning beach. The 80m (262ft) long tunnel is submerged at High Water, so the beach is only accessible at certain times of the day, and only at Low Water to small boats.

Krabi: The only mainland port of any size within this destination is Krabi. Lying 55nm east of Phuket, it offers some stunning beaches and is popular with the climbing fraternity. The limestone stacks near Krabi provide some of the best climbing in the world, to suit a variety of skill levels. You'll also find two marinas plus good facilities.

Koh Khao Phing Kan: No visit to Phang Nga Bay is complete without a visit to this iconic island. Famed for its filmic associations and its English name, James Bond Island, Koh Khao Phing Kan is immediately recognizable for the tooth-like projection that juts out of the emerald green waters that surround it. Both Koh Khao Phing Kan and the nearby Koh Tapu, or Nail Island, appeared in the 1974 Bond film *The Man With the Golden Gun*. Soaring to 20m (66ft) above sea level, the island forms part of the Phang Nga National Park.

Level of skill

You don't need a lot of experience to sail this route. Consistent winds of between 5 and 20 knots from the northeast are the norm from November to April, which makes for delightful sailing conditions. During the wet season, which runs from May to October, wind strengths are similar, although they can be stronger at times. However, as the cruising area is in relatively protected waters this does not pose a problem.

Tidal range within Phang Nga Bay and the surrounding area is 2–3m, so bear this in mind when laying your anchor. Tidal currents generally run at about 2 knots, apart from in the narrow channels between some of the islands where they can be stronger, so care should be taken.

When navigating, watch out for unmarked reefs and patches of coral lying off the islands. As the area is a popular tourist destination you should also watch out for other boats. Numerous longtails – the traditional fishing and tourist boats powered by car or bus engines perched precariously on the stern – ply these waters. It is important to be vigilant, although they are so noisy that you will usually hear them before you see them.

Some anchorages can get crowded during the day, so choose your spot carefully. Many of the anchorages are shallow, so deep-draught yachts will need to anchor well off. Even shallow-draught catamarans will have to plan their stopover if they run themselves up the beach, as they may end up far from the edge of the sea at Low Water. In some places, such as Ao Chalong at Phuket, the bays dry extensively at Low Water, so tide times should be checked before going ashore. Most of the anchorages offer good holding on sand or mud and are relatively sheltered from the prevailing winds.

When to go

One of the delights of cruising in Thailand is that there is no specific sailing season, so you are not restricted to visiting at a particular time of year. Thailand enjoys a tropical climate, and although it is affected by monsoon weather, it is not severe enough to prevent year-round sailing.

Temperatures are fairly consistent, averaging 25–30°C (77–86°F) throughout the year, with March to May being the hottest months. As the southwest monsoon kicks in between May and October, so does the rain, and September and October are generally wet and humid, often recording up to 356mm (14in) of rain. November to March is typically the dry season, with minimal rain, and a preferred time to visit by many sailors owing to the stable northeasterly winds that average between 5 and 20 knots. The area covered by this route is, however, relatively sheltered and protected, and although stronger winds occur at times, they are usually short-lived and not severe enough to cause problems. Year-round sailing here is therefore possible.

PHUKET AND PHANG NGA BAY AT A GLANCE

Route length: Around 192nm.

Time required: Two to three weeks.

When to go: Any time, although November to March offers the best sailing conditions, with less chance of rain.

Weather: Tropical climate with minimal fluctuation of temperatures throughout the year. Average temperatures are 25–30°C (77–86°F) with the hottest months being March to May. Winds are usually 5–20 knots during the northeasterly monsoon, between November and March. September and October are the wettest months. Water temperature is usually around 28°C (82°F).

Type and size of boat: Power or sail, 25ft (7.6m) plus. Many of the bays are shallow, so shoal-draught is preferable, as it means you can get closer inshore or run up the sandy beaches.

Equipment: Basic navigation equipment, a decent anchor, snorkelling or diving gear.

Tides: Tidal range of 2–3m. Tidal currents usually run at a maximum of 2 knots, although they may run faster in narrow channels between the islands, where care should be taken.

Hazards: No major hazards, but watch out for unmarked reefs and patches of coral. Can get busy with other boats, so maintain a good lookout at all times.

Suitable for night sailing: Yes, with care.

Difficulty of route: Easy to moderate.

Skills required: Ability to anchor, taking into account the rise and fall of tides, plus manoeuvring in crowded anchorages.

Charts: Admiralty: 3941 (Mu Ko Similan to Koh Lanta Yai). Royal Thai Navy charts.

Berthing/mooring: Four marinas to choose from at Phuket Town on Phuket Island, and two more to choose from at Krabi on the mainland, 55nm to the east. Berthing is generally stern- or bow-to. There is a huge choice of anchorages along the route.

Ports of entry: Phuket Town on Phuket Island and Krabi on the mainland.

Water: Available from all the marinas. There are limited provisions on the islands.

Provisioning: Available at Phuket Town and Krabi. There are limited provisions on the islands.

Fuel: Available at Phuket Town and Krabi.

Shorepower: Available at Phuket Town and Krabi.

Maintenance: Boatyard facilities are available at all the marinas at Phuket Town, and some at Krabi. Facilities are improving as the area becomes more popular.

Family friendliness: This area is very family orientated. Some of the world's finest beaches can be found in this area, and with crystal-clear waters there is plenty of snorkelling too. Krabi is good for older children interested in climbing.

Further reading: *South-East Asia Pilot* (Imray).

left Krabi, on the mainland coast of Thailand, has great beaches as well as plenty of places to climb on limestone stacks.

VOYAGE 21

The Indian Ocean

THE SEYCHELLES

There aren't many locations around the world that offer a year-round sailing season. The position of the Seychelles, 930nm east of Africa, makes this possible. Located northeast of the island of Madagascar, this archipelago boasts some of the most stunning cruising grounds in the world. It comprises over 100 islands, with the archipelago divided into two distinct groups – the Inner Islands and the Outer Islands.

For cruising sailors the Inner Islands hold the most attraction and are home to the main island of Mahé and most of the facilities within the area. The Outer Islands, which lie at a distance of between 130nm and 630nm miles off Mahé, are more exposed to the prevailing conditions and are surrounded by low-lying reefs and coral atolls, making sailing more difficult.

Within the Inner Islands you will find true paradise. The area is starting to become more popular with cruising boats and charter companies but remains idyllic through much of the archipelago. The wildlife and fauna here is incredible – giant tortoises and crabs wander around many of the islands, while offshore the seas teem with a huge abundance of marine life. The islands of Praslin and Curieuse are also the only places in the world that you will find the Coco de Mer palm, also called the sea coconut. It grows up to 30m (98ft) in height and bears extraordinary looking fruit that can weigh up to 42kg (93lb).

Sailing within the Inner Islands is effortless. Distances between the islands are small and conditions well suited to people of most abilities so it is hard to be disappointed here.

below The main island within the Inner Islands is Mahé, which has some stunning anchorages.

The route

The route is a circular circumnavigation of some of the 43 islands that comprise the Inner group of the Seychelles Archipelago. The start and endpoint is the island of Mahé and its capital Victoria, which lies on the northeastern coast. The island offers numerous places to explore and a clockwise circumnavigation is recommended before exploring the rest of the archipelago. Places to visit include the Ste-Anne Marine National Park, due east of Victoria, as well as Anse Royale on the southeastern tip of the island. From here, continue around the island to the northwestern coast, where there are a number of delightful anchorages, including Anse à la Mouche, Baie Ternay, Anse du Riz, Anse Major and Anse Beau Vallon.

From the north coast of Mahé make a 23nm hop to the twin islands of Cousine and Cousin, which lie off the southwestern coast of Praslin. From Cousin, head to Baie Chevalier and Anse Lazio on the northern tip of Praslin, before continuing northeast to the island of Curieuse. Baie Laraie on the east coast provides the next destination, before heading back to Praslin and

anchorages at Anse Possession on the north coast and Anse La Farine on the east coast. After that, head east for 6nm to the island of La Digue.

The first port of call on La Digue is Anse La Reunion on the island's west coast, before heading north to La Passe, where you will find all-weather anchorages. Continue clockwise round the island before heading to the island of Félicité, which lies around 4nm to the northeast. If you like, a daytime anchorage can be found at Grande Anse on the east coast of Grande Soeur, a privately owned island. Overnighting is not permitted here so return to La Digue and the anchorage at Anse Cocos on the southeastern tip of the island. Continue clockwise round La Digue and you will reach Anse Source d'Argent, which is said to be the world's most photographed beach, and Anse Union. From here, head southwest back to Victoria on Mahé.

below There are numerous beaches and smaller islets to explore in this region.

Destinations

Mahé: The largest island in this archipelago is home to over 85 per cent of the country's population and there is plenty of coastline to explore. Some of the finest anchorages in this group of islands can be found here, and with excellent facilities in the form of marinas, boatyards, shops and restaurants it has much to offer. There are also many beaches to explore. Victoria is the island's main destination and the capital of the Seychelles. First established by the French in 1778, it is named after Queen Victoria after the British took over possession of the colony in 1812. Independent since 1976, French, English and Creole are the languages now spoken here.

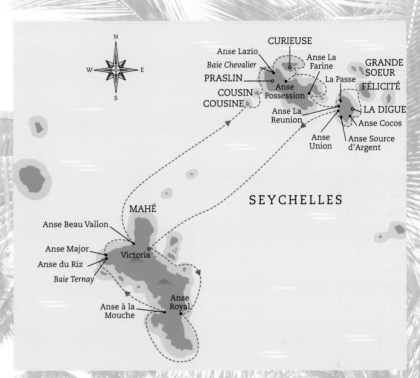

Praslin: The second-largest island in the Inner Seychelles group, Praslin is a fascinating place to explore. It is also stunning, with several very good anchorages fringed by white-sand beaches and pinky-red granite rocks. Ashore you'll find the UNESCO World Heritage Site of the Vallée de Mai Nature Reserve, one of only two places in the world where the Coco de Mer palm grows. The wildlife here is incredible and the island is well worth exploring on foot.

Curieuse: Lying off the northeast coast of Praslin, Curieuse is distinctive for its red soil and was once known as Ile Rouge (Red Island). The giant tortoise is a great focus of attention and there are now said to be over 500 on the island as well as an active breeding programme with the Curieuse National Marine Park. Aside from Praslin, this is also the only other place in the world where Coco de Mer palms grow.

La Digue: This idyllic island is home to one of the world's rarest birds – the black paradise flycatcher. All cars are banned here and consequently the pace of life is somewhat slower. La Passe and its nearby anchorages are the main draw for visiting boats but the glorious white-sand beach of Anse Source d'Argent is a popular location, as one of the world's most famous beaches. The fauna and flora here is stunning and forays ashore to explore are much recommended.

Level of skill

You don't need to be a highly skilled sailor to enjoy this cruising area. Unlike the remote Outer Islands, which are exposed and formed of numerous reef-fringed, low-lying islands in potentially tricky and shallow waters, the Inner group is reasonably protected and hazard-free. There are still plenty of rocks to watch out for and you should take care when in anchorages where coral is prevalent, but generally the sailing is fairly relaxed. However, it is not advisable to sail around the islands at night.

Winds in this area blow from the northwest from November through to April, whereas from May to October they blow from the southeast. The windiest months tend to be between December and March, although with average wind speeds rarely in excess of 20 knots, this does not make for particularly challenging conditions.

The tidal range within the archipelago is usually between 0.9 and 2m, and it is worth studying your chart carefully before anchoring, as some bays can dry completely at Low Water. Tidal currents run at 0.5–2 knots, with stronger currents running in some of the inter-island channels.

Anchoring here is straightforward on sand in depths of 5–8m. Watch out for patches of coral, as anchoring on coral is forbidden and fines are imposed if you breach these rules. Some of the bays along the route require visiting boats to anchor within particular zones to protect either the marine environment or swimmers and snorkellers, so consult your charts before dropping the hook.

In previous years, this part of the Indian Ocean has been in the news with stories of piracy. In 2009 Paul and Rachel Chandler were held hostage by Somali pirates for 388 days after their boat was boarded 60nm off Victoria on Mahé. Although reports of piracy in this area have declined in recent years it is worth seeking expert advice if you intend to cruise west of the Seychelles.

When to go

Located outside the cyclone belt, the Seychelles enjoy a settled and predictable climate, which makes the inner archipelago suitable for sailing year-round. What defines the two seasons – May to October and November to April – is the direction of the prevailing winds. From November to April, northwesterly trade winds prevail, along with the probability of higher humidity and more rain. January and February tend to be the wettest months while April and November are the most settled in terms of temperature, wind strengths and sea conditions. Between May and October, the southeasterly trade winds blow in, and with them drier conditions arrive. Temperatures average between 24 and 32°C (75 and 90°F).

The Seychelles are busiest with tourists between December and January and July and August, but a wide choice of anchorages and things to do ashore means that even in peak season you can still find pockets of seclusion.

THE SEYCHELLES AT A GLANCE

Route length: Around 200nm.

Time required: Three weeks. You need longer if you also want to explore the Outer Islands.

When to go: Year-round, although the best months are March and April, October and November.

Weather: Tropical climate. November to April: northwest tradewinds; May to October: southeast tradewinds. Average temperatures 24–32°C (75–90°F). January and February are the wettest months, while April and November usually offer the most settled conditions.

Type and size of boat: Power or sail, 25ft (7.6m) plus.

Equipment: Charts, chartplotter, depth sounder, binoculars, decent anchor, snorkelling gear, reliable engine.

Tides: Tidal range among the Inner Islands is 0.9–2m. Currents average 0.5–2 knots.

Hazards: Lots of unmarked rocks, coral, low-lying islands, swimmers and snorkellers.

Suitable for night sailing: No, not at all. The hazards detailed above and the fact that most are unmarked mean that sailing within close proximity of the islands at night is not advised.

Difficulty of route: Moderate.

Skills required: Good navigation and pilotage skills and the ability to anchor.

Charts: Admiralty: 721 (Southern Approaches to the Seychelles Group), 740 (The Seychelles Group), 742 (Mahé, Praslin and adjacent islands), 722 (Port Victoria and Approaches), 724 (Anchorages in the Seychelles Group and outlying islands).

Berthing/mooring: Mahé: The Wharf Marina; Eden Island Marina; Seychelles YC; Angel Fish Marina. None of the other islands have marinas. There are moorings off the northwest coast of Mahé, and at La Digue and Praslin. There is also a huge choice of anchorages.

Ports of entry: Victoria on Mahé.

Water: From marinas on Mahé. Available from Baie St Anne on Praslin and La Passe on La Digue by prior arrangement.

Provisioning: Victoria on Mahé is the main provisioning destination. There are some shops on Praslin and La Digue, but they are limited in other parts of the archipelago.

Fuel: Available from marinas on Mahé.

Shorepower: Available from marinas on Mahé.

Maintenance: Range of boatyard facilities at Victoria on Mahé, so if you need to make repairs or find someone to service your engine, this is the place to visit. None of the other islands offer facilities.

Family friendliness: Very family friendly, but caution in the area west of Seychelles is required, owing to acts of piracy off the Somali coast in recent years.

Further reading: *Indian Ocean Cruising Guide* by Rod Heikell; *Seychelles Nautical Pilot* by Alain Rondeau.

left The giant tortoise is one of the main attractions on the island of Curieuse.

VOYAGE 22
New Zealand

AUCKLAND AND THE BAY OF ISLANDS

The eastern coast of New Zealand's North Island boasts some of the finest cruising grounds in the country. Rich in cultural history and diverse in scenery, the coastline north of Auckland offers a variety of destinations that will cater for all. Auckland, the departure point of this cruise, has much to offer especially if you're looking for a vibrant city that is passionate about yachting as well as its nightlife and cultural sites.

Alternatively, if it's quiet wilderness, peaceful anchorages and diverse wildlife that you are seeking, then you'll find this too by exploring the many bays, islands and inlets along this coastline.

Both the Hauraki Gulf, on which Auckland stands, and the Bay of Islands, the final destination on this route, will vie for your attention, offering myriad places to stop for lunch or overnight. The Bay of Islands' name gives a clue to the type of geography that you will discover here, for there are 144 islands within its circumference. The Hauraki Gulf is home to over 50 islands, many of which can be visited by boat, although others are conservation sites and offer restricted access only.

Whangarei Harbour, which lies about 80nm north of Auckland, is a worthy destination too. Home to a major yachting centre and a huge array of facilities including four marinas, it's a popular port of call and is set in a picturesque location. To the north, Whangaruru Harbour offers a quieter alternative.

Steady, predictable winds and a sunny temperate climate make New Zealand's eastern coast hard to beat. The hardest thing on this cruise will be finding time to fit everything in.

below There are over 144 islands within the Bay of Islands, the final destination of this fascinating cruise.

The route

This linear cruise encompasses at least three of New Zealand's finest cruising grounds: the Hauraki Gulf, Whangarei and the Bay of Islands. Starting in Auckland, the first port of call within the Hauraki Gulf is Motuihe, to the northeast, before heading northwest to Rangitoto Island. From there, head north to Tiritiri Matangi Island before continuing to Kawau Island, and then east and around the Coromandel Peninsula to Whitianga. The route then continues northwest to Great Barrier Island, a stunning destination that stands guard over the entrance to the Hauraki Gulf.

From here, the route hugs the island coastline before heading northwest to Whangarei Harbour. This large and picturesque harbour is a major boating centre with excellent facilities. Continuing northwards, the next main stop is Whangaruru Harbour. Smaller than Whangarei, the harbour offers some delightful anchorages off sandy beaches in sheltered waters and is usually quieter, with fewer visitors than other nearby harbours.

Cape Brett marks the easternmost headland at the entrance to the Bay of Islands. It's identifiable by its white lighthouse and the famous 'hole in the rock' formation, which motorboats can pass through with care if there isn't too much swell in the vicinity. Once inside the headland the whole bay and its 144 islands will open up before you. The Ninepin, 11nm to the west of Cape Brett, marks the bay's westernmost headland.

Anchorages and islands to visit abound here and you could easily spend a week or two exploring. Take your time before heading back south to Auckland or north to experience the delights of the northlands.

below Auckland is often considered the yachting capital of the southern hemisphere.

Destinations

Auckland: Home to eight large marinas, Auckland's nickname 'City of Sails' says it all. The city lives, breathes and sleeps boats, with boats numbering more per head than anywhere else in the world. As a starting destination it is hard to beat: everything you need or want is within easy reach, and for those that want to experience some cultural highlights, there is much to see and do. Notable sights include the Voyager New Zealand Maritime Museum, the Auckland Museum and the 328m (1,076ft) high Sky Tower.

Hauraki Gulf: This 4,000sq km (1,544 square mile) inlet is a yachtsman's delight. There are over 200 anchorages to choose from to suit a variety of wind and swell conditions. Ashore, the gulf is home to the Hauraki Gulf Marine Park, within which are five marine reserves. Try to visit Rangitoto Island, just north of Auckland, formed from a 600-year-old dormant volcano. Attached via a causeway to Rangitoto is Motutapu Island. Sites of interest here include World War II bunkers and tunnels, as well as some stunning views across the Hauraki Gulf. Motuihe Island, to the southeast, has some fabulous beaches and indigenous heritage sites, Tiritiri Matangi Island is recommended for its incredible wildlife, while Kawau Island, one of the largest in the gulf, has some beautiful, sheltered anchorages and an interesting history. Mahurangi Harbour is part of a tidal estuary, with boatyard facilities at Warkworth. On the eastern coast of the Coromandel Peninsula there is Mercury Bay and the harbour of Whitianga, which is home to the Mercury Bay Boating Club. Crystal-clear waters, tranquil beaches and rugged beauty define Great Barrier Island, which stands guard over the entrance to the Hauraki Gulf and is packed with wildlife and stunning walks.

Whangarei: In Maori, the name means 'place where whales gather', and all year round minke, humpback,

pilot, Bryde's and southern right whales can be seen in these waters. The harbour itself offers numerous facilities for visiting boats. The Poor Knights Islands, 30nm northeast of Bream Head, are also worth a visit if you are interested in diving.

Bay of Islands: Known as the 'Gateway to New Zealand', the Bay of Islands is one of the most popular destinations on the eastern coast, and you really are spoilt for choice here when it comes to destinations. Opua, located in the southern corner of the bay, is the main deep-water port and home to an excellent marina. Paihia to the north is very touristy, so head instead to Russell, to the northeast, if you need to re-provision. Anchorages can be found everywhere, but the best area is within the Te Rawhiti Inlet, which lies to the northeast of Russell, and the mainland coast to the southeast of it, where shelter from all conditions can usually be found in secluded bays. Opito Bay, near Kerikeri, on the northwestern coast of the Keriteri Inlet, is also recommended. There is a marina at Kerikeri, as well as New Zealand's oldest building at the head of the creek.

Level of skill

You don't need any particular skills to cruise the east coast of New Zealand. Basic navigation and pilotage skills are necessary for the main part of the route, but in general it is hazard-free. Winds in this area during the sailing season are usually quite settled and from a westerly direction.

The biggest hazards in most of these cruising areas are other boats. The Auckland area and the Hauraki Gulf can both get very busy during peak season with motorboats, yachts, daytripper boats and ferries. The stunning cruising grounds of the Bay of Islands make it very popular too, so maintaining a good lookout is essential at all times.

Watch out for unmarked rocks and islets, particularly near the islands or headlands, and for tidal eddies too. Currents between the islands can be strong, particularly in areas where the channels are narrow, such as near the Coromandel Peninsula in the Hauraki Gulf. Tidal ranges here are between 1.9 and 2.9m, while in the Bay of Islands they are around 2m.

A good, practical knowledge of anchoring is useful, although there are plenty of marinas and moorings available along the route too. However, the beauty of this area is that if one anchorage proves untenable, there are likely to be more suitable alternatives available close by.

When to go

New Zealand enjoys a temperate climate, and is popular with sailors all year round. The sailing season, however, tends to run during the summer months, from November to April, when temperatures are higher and the rain probability is lower.

The Bay of Islands, about 100nm north of Auckland, has an almost subtropical climate, and on average temperatures are higher here than in New Zealand's capital city. The Bay receives more sunshine too, with westerly (southwesterly through to northwesterly) Force 1–4 winds prevailing.

During the winter months New Zealand can be wet and windy, with July experiencing the coolest temperatures. In Auckland these average around 11°C (52°F), but during the summer months (November to April) temperatures range from 20°C to 30°C (68°F to 86°F).

AUCKLAND AND THE BAY OF ISLANDS AT A GLANCE

Route length: Approximately 170nm.

Time required: At least three weeks, more if possible.

When to go: November to April.

Weather: A temperate climate that is warmer in the north. Dry and warm conditions prevail from November to April, with westerly winds ranging from Force 1 to 4. The Bay of Islands' more northerly location means that temperatures here are generally higher and on average range between 20 and 30°C (68 and 86°F).

Type and size of boat: Power or sail, 25ft (7.6m) plus.

Equipment: Standard navigation equipment, including charts, chartplotter, depth sounder and GPS, as well as a good anchor.

Tides: The tidal range in the Bay of Islands is 2m, while in the Hauraki Gulf it is 1.9–2.9m. There are strong currents in the narrow channels between the islands and around some headlands.

Hazards: Ferries and daytripper boats, unmarked rocks and tidal eddies.

Suitable for night sailing: Yes, many of the main hazards on this route are lit at night, and although caution should be exercised in the Bay of Islands, the coastal cruise from Auckland to the Bay of Islands offers few night-time hazards.

Difficulty of route: Easy to moderate.

Skills required: No specific skills are required other than basic pilotage, navigation and anchoring skills.

Charts: Admiralty: 4640 (New Zealand North Island), 4641 (Norfolk Island to Cape Egmont), 4600 (New Zealand).

Berthing/mooring: Marinas in all the major harbours: Auckland, Whangarei, Opua, plus countless anchoring opportunities.

Ports of entry: Auckland, Whangarei, Opua.

Water: Available at all major towns and marinas.

Provisioning: Widely available at towns and villages throughout the route. Auckland offers the best choice, and if you can't find what you want here then you won't find it anywhere. Opua and Whangarei are also good options.

Fuel: Available at all marinas.

Shorepower: Available at all marinas.

Maintenance: Auckland, Whangarei and the Bay of Islands have facilities for repairs and maintenance. Most marinas have full facilities.

Family friendliness: Very family friendly. Lots of things for children to see and do, particularly in Auckland, where museums and activities abound.

Further reading: *Destination NZ: Blue Water Cruisers Guide, New Zealand's Northern Waters* by Graham Brice and Christopher Carey; *Coastal Cruising Handbook* by Royal Arkana Yacht Club; *Landfalls of Paradise: Cruising Guide to the Pacific Islands* by Earl R Hinz and Jim Howard.

left Mercury Bay lies on the east coast of the Coromandel Peninsula, to the east of Auckland.

VOYAGE 23

Australia

THE WHITSUNDAY ISLANDS

Discovered by Captain James Cook in 1770, this group of islands, which lie off the northeast coast of Queensland in Australia, is considered to offer some of the best cruising in the world. Brilliant turquoise waters, white sandy beaches, lush, densely wooded islands and secluded anchorages among the coral abound. And if the landscape does not make you smile in awe, the wildlife certainly will.

Lying close to the Great Barrier Reef – the largest coral reef system in the world – the Whitsunday Islands offer a huge and diverse variety of species of fish and birds. From June to September they are a nursery and playground for young humpback and pilot whales moving en route to more northerly waters. Scuba diving and snorkelling is a must. Although this area is home to the South Pacific's largest bareboat charter fleet, there are quiet anchorages and isolated beaches, particularly if you visit the less popular, uninhabited islands to the south.

The sailing conditions here are superb too, with steady 15–20-knot southeasterly trade winds being the norm. Although navigating and anchoring among the coral-fringed islands can appear daunting and certainly requires a high degree of skill, it is not an area restricted to experienced sailors only.

The whole of the Whitsunday Islands is a national park, so be aware that there are a number of regulations enforced, including where you can anchor, where you can fish and the disposal of rubbish. But the reasons for the regulations becomes abundantly clear when you experience this wonderful cruising area.

below Much of Hook Island is thickly wooded, with beautiful coral-fringed beaches along Butterfly Bay.

The route

The route suggested for this destination is circular and starts from Abell Point Marina near Airlie Beach, one of the primary jumping off locations for exploring the Whitsunday Islands. From there, head northeast for around 24nm to Butterfly Bay on the northeastern coast of Hook Island. You can either sail 13nm to the spectacularly stunning Nara Inlet on the southern coast of the island, or take a detour via Langford Island, which lies to the west, two miles south of Hayman Island.

From Hayman Island, head back to Nara Inlet and its twin, Maconna, on the southern coast of Hook Island, before heading east around the northeastern tip of Whitsunday Island to Cataran Bay on Border Island. For anyone wishing to go to the Great Barrier Reef, Border Island or the northeastern tip of Hook Island are the closest to the most westerly part, Hook Reef.

From Border Island, head south to the largest island: Whitsunday Island. Whitehaven Beach is the most

above The aquamarine sea and white sand of Whitehaven Beach make it definitely worth a visit.

popular destination, 8½nm away, but Turtle Bay on the southern coast is also well worth a visit. Haslewood Island immediately to the east is the next destination, via the Solway Passage, before the route heads south to Shaw Island. Numerous anchorages can be found here, as well as a resort at Billbob Bay.

Lindeman Island lies 16nm south of Hamilton Island and is the next port of call, with a good anchorage at Plantation Bay, before the route heads to Hamilton Island, the capital of the archipelago. Six nautical miles to the west lies Long Island and anchorages at Happy Bay or Palm Bay. From there you can head either to Shute Harbour, immediately to the northwest on the mainland, or back to Abell Point Marina, 11nm to the north.

Destinations

Airlie Beach: The first port of call on this route is the tourist destination of Airlie Beach. As the gateway to the Whitsunday Islands it is busy peak season, but facilities at Abell Point Marina are excellent so it is a good place to start your cruise.

Hook Island: Approximately 13nm northeast of Abell Point Marina is Hook Island. The island is thickly wooded with twin fjord-like inlets, Nara and Maconna, on its southern coast. Both provide good all-weather anchorages, while ashore you can discover early Aboriginal cave paintings as well as waterfalls and good walks. Butterfly Bay, on the northeastern corner of the island, is also worth a visit. The bay has some visitors' moorings but care should be taken when anchoring as coral abounds.

Border Island: This Y-shaped rocky island lies to the southeast of Hook Island and is uninhabited. Dramatic cliffs line its eastern coast, but Cataran Bay on its northern coast offers a good anchorage, although it should be avoided in strong winds as short 'bullet' gusts are regularly experienced. It is quiet so it is a good place for experiencing marine life. Walks on the mountains ashore will provide good views of the archipelago.

Great Barrier Reef: Few people can dispute the incredible beauty of the Great Barrier Reef. This World Heritage Site is the world's largest coral reef, and includes over 3,000 individual reef systems and 900 islands, and spans about 344,400sq km (132,974 square miles) of sea, 34nm east of the Queensland coast. An incredible diversity of species makes this a fantastic destination for scuba diving and snorkelling.

Whitsunday Island: The largest island in the archipelago, Whitsunday Island is best known for its stunning white silica sands. Whitehaven Beach, one of the world's top beaches, is located on the southeastern corner of the island. It really is idyllic, but it can get busy in peak season. Turtle Bay on the southern coast of the island is a good alternative.

Haslewood Island: If you cross the Solway Passage, which lies to the east of Whitsunday Island, you will reach Haslewood Island. Chalkies Beach on its northwestern shore offers a good alternative to Whitehaven Beach – it has the same white, silky smooth sandy beach but fewer visitors.

Shaw Island: Due south of Haslewood Island lies Shaw Island, one of the biggest in the archipelago. It is home to a large resort, which visiting boats are welcome to use for a fee. Care should be taken on approach to Billbob Bay owing to the numerous bommies (outcrops of coral reef), overfalls and eddies that line the entrance.

Lindeman Island: Covered by eucalyptus, this island is dominated by a resort, although the facilities can be used by visiting boats for a fee. The anchorage at Plantation Bay on the southern coast is lovely and usually relatively quiet too.

Hamilton Island: Hamilton Island is the capital and most densely populated of the islands. It boasts an airport and a 245-berth marina with full boatyard facilities. It is also home to several charter fleets, so expect it to be busy peak season. Anchorages can be found in Cid Harbour, which lies between Cid Island and Whitsunday Island off the northwestern coast of Hamilton Island.

Level of skill

You don't need to be an expert to sail these waters, but you do need to know how to anchor your boat properly. Most of the anchorages are fringed by coral reefs, which must be avoided at all costs. Anchoring on coral breaches the national park's regulations, and you may receive a fine for damaging it.

All the anchorages available within the Whitsunday Islands offer varying degrees of shelter depending on wind conditions and direction. Many are susceptible to localized gusts of wind that can disappear almost as quickly as they appear, but can play havoc if you're not anchored securely.

Large tidal ranges within the islands, up to 3m in height, also mean that you must lay the correct amount of scope for the rise and fall of the tides when anchoring. These huge tidal ranges can also cause problems in many of the passages in between the islands, some of which, such as the Solway Passage between Whitsunday Island and Haslewood Island, are particularly narrow. Expect to find fast-running currents and turbulence in this area when the tide is at maximum flood and ebb, and avoid them in wind-over-tide conditions. Watch out for eddies and overfalls around some of the islands' headlands too.

Generally, the sailing conditions here are superb, and suitable for most abilities. The waters are protected by the Great Barrier Reef, which helps moderate and stabilize wind and sea conditions in the archipelago.

In terms of navigation it is also relatively easy, and eyeball navigation is all that is required. The turquoise waters are crystal clear so you should be able to identify any hazards before you go over them, provided a good lookout is maintained at all times. There are plenty of unmarked reefs and coral heads throughout the route, and most of the islands are reef- or coral-fringed so particular care must be taken when entering any bays or harbours. However, if one bay proves unsuitable for any reason, another stunning anchorage is always just round the corner only a short sail away.

When to go

The weather in the Whitsundays is a typical warm subtropical climate, with warm/hot summers and mild winters. January to March are the wettest months, but by the time the sailing season begins in April rain is generally a distant memory. Expect temperatures to average 22–23°C (72–73°F) in June and July and 29–30°C (84–86°F) during December and January.

Scuba diving and snorkelling is a major attraction within the islands, and the water temperature is usually around 25°C (77°F). During the sailing season winds average 15–20 knots, and although cyclones can hit this part of the Queensland coast they normally occur from November to May.

The Whitsunday Islands are hugely popular, so during the season expect to encounter lots of charter boats. However, the size of the archipelago and the sheer number of destinations within it mean that it is still possible to find secluded anchorages and remote, uninhabited parts of the islands, even in peak season.

THE WHITSUNDAY ISLANDS AT A GLANCE

Route length: Approximately 130nm, although it will vary according to which islands you visit.

Time required: Two weeks.

When to go: April to October.

Weather: Mild winters and warm summers characterize the Whitsunday Islands' subtropical climate.

Type and size of boat: Power or sail, 25ft (7.6m) plus.

Equipment: Charts, depth sounder, decent anchor, diving and snorkelling gear.

Tides: The Whitsunday Islands experience big tides, with a range of 3–4m. On a flooding tide the current moves south, and on an ebbing tide the current moves north.

Hazards: Strong currents (up to 5 knots in places), eddies and overfalls in some of the channels between the islands and around headlands, reefs and bommies, sandbanks, coral, bullet gusts in some of the bays.

Suitable for night sailing: No, many of the bays are littered with coral, bommies and unmarked reefs, which means that safe night passages are very tricky.

Difficulty of route: Moderate.

Skills required: Excellent anchoring skills are essential. Basic pilotage skills required too, as well as the ability to maintain a good lookout.

Charts: Admiralty: AUS0252 (Whitsunday Group), AUS0824 (Penrith Island to Whitsunday Island), AUS0825 (Whitsunday Island to Bowen).

Berthing/mooring: Abell Point Marina at Airlie Beach and Hamilton Island Marina, Hamilton Island.

Ports of entry: Mackay Harbour, Queensland, to the south of the Whitsunday Islands.

Water: Available at Abell Point Marina, Airlie Beach, and at Hamilton Island Marina, Hamilton Island.

Provisioning: Most provisions are available at Airlie Beach, but you need to plan your provisioning in advance. Some companies operate a victualling service to charter yachts. You make a food order and they deliver direct to your boat.

Fuel: Available at Abell Point Marina, Airlie Beach, and at Hamilton Island Marina, Hamilton Island.

Shorepower: Available at Abell Point Marina, Airlie Beach, and at Hamilton Island Marina, Hamilton Island.

Maintenance: Boatyard facilities at Hamilton Island Marina and Abell Point Marina, Airlie Beach.

Family friendliness: Very family friendly.

Further reading: *100 Magic Miles of Great Barrier Reef: The Whitsunday Islands* by David Colfelt; *Whitsundays Book* by David Colfelt; *Cruising the Coral Coast* by Alan Lucas.

left Scuba diving or snorkelling on the Great Barrier Reef reveals incredible marine life.

VOYAGE 24 IF YOU WANT A CHALLENGE

The Pacific Ocean

THE COOK ISLANDS

Only around 150 yachts visit the Cook Islands each year. This group of 15 islands, which are located in the South Pacific Ocean between French Polynesia and Fiji, northeast of New Zealand, are formed of 241sq km (93 square miles) of land scattered over an expanse of sea that extends for 1,787sq km (690 square miles).

The Cook Islands are a very remote archipelago, divided into two distinct groups, the Northern and the Southern groups. Six coral atolls – ancient volcanoes that have long since sunk below the sea, with only the coral-fringed tips evident – form the Northern group. Of these, Penrhyn is the largest and most remote of all the Cook Islands, lying 737nm north-northwest of the island of Rarotonga, the administrative capital of the archipelago, which forms part of the Southern group.

Nine islands and atolls comprise the Southern Cook Islands, which lie fairly close to each other. These lush, fertile islands are home to most of the Cook islanders. They were first discovered in the late 18th century when Captain James Cook, after whom the islands were later named, visited during his second voyage from 1773 to 1775. These islands now form the main focus for cruising boats exploring this area and offer a dazzling snapshot of real paradise. High mountains densely covered in vegetation dominate the islands while their coastlines are fringed with incredible turquoise blue waters and sparkling white sands.

Sailing here is not easy; the islands' remoteness and the large distances between them means that passages need to be planned with care. However, the rewards are very rich indeed.

below The stunning aquamarine seas of the Cook Islands make them an idyllic place to visit.

The route

Although the whole archipelago of 15 islands and atolls are worth exploring, the distances between them are huge, which makes the practicalities of doing so tricky. Cruising within the Cook Islands requires a permit, which lasts for 31 days before it must be renewed. This means that it is not possible to fully explore both the Southern and the Northern groups within a month. Therefore, the route detailed below covers only the Southern group with a circular cruise lasting three to four weeks, covering over 900nm.

The starting point is Rarotonga, the largest island in the archipelago. You will find the best facilities for cruising boats here at Avatiu, the main port. It is also possible to anchor off the island, although it is worth contacting the port authority for information before attempting to do so. From Avatiu, head 270nm northwest to the atoll island of Palmerston. It is important to check the weather before making this passage as it is exposed, and the moorings at Palmerston are not tenable if conditions deteriorate with strong winds from the north or west.

From Palmerston atoll, head to Aitutaki, 200nm to the east-southeast. The entrance channel to the lagoon here is narrow and quite shallow, but access for boats drawing up to 1.8m is available. Larger boats should anchor off. Next sail 53nm sail east-southeast to Manuae, an uninhabited atoll, where you can also anchor off. From here, head east-southeast again for 80nm to Mitiaro, before sailing 27nm southeast to Mauke, the 'garden of the islands'.

Lying 44nm east of Mauke you will find Atiu or Enuamamu, a fascinating raised volcanic island, before the route heads south to Mangaia. This is the second-largest Cook Island and the most southern, 116nm south of Atiu. The circumnavigation of the islands then reaches its conclusion back at Rarotonga, 112nm to the northwest.

Destinations

Rarotonga: This island is the main destination of visitors to the Cook Islands. Home to over 13,000 people, the island is the biggest within the Southern group at 67sq km (26 square miles). Volcanic in origin, the island is enclosed by a lagoon, with four coral islets lying off Muri Beach on its southeastern coast. The principal port of the island and the only real commercial harbour within the Cook Islands is Avatiu, which lies on the northern coast of the island and to the east of the international airport. Here, you will find maintenance, fuel, water, gas, limited chandlery (although spares can be imported in here from New Zealand), as well as provisions. You can moor in stern- or bow-to berths on the quay. However, while the harbour is good for provisions and facilities, it is susceptible to swell. Ashore, you can trek around the island and its peaks, go mountain biking or visit local villages. Snorkelling in the crystal-clear turquoise waters is a dream.

Palmerston atoll: Visitors to Palmerston atoll are certainly well looked after. A local tradition has run for many years whereby the family of the owner of the mooring you pick up on arrival will look after you for the duration of your stay. The moorings can be exposed in northerly or westerly winds, but the hospitality is superb; the families will feed you and let you use their facilities, such as showers and washing machines. Formed of six islets, Palmerston atoll is also lush with vegetation and abundant marine life.

Aitutaki: The narrowness and shallowness of the channel that leads to the small boat harbour and lagoon on the island of Aitutaki may be off-putting to visitors, but when you get there you will find a superb anchorage – one of the best in the Cook Islands. Sheltered and flat calm, the harbour is a total contrast to Rarotonga. Although its provisions and facilities are limited, it's an idyllic place to spend some time.

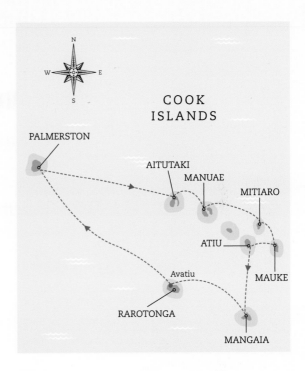

Manuae: This was the first island to be sighted by Captain James Cook in 1773, and was once home to around 600 people and a penal colony. Now uninhabited, it is abundant with marine and island wildlife and is beautifully unspoilt as it receives very few visitors each year.

Atiu: The third largest island in the archipelago, Atiu is delightfully remote and unspoilt. If you're interested in birdwatching, then this island is a real haven as birdlife flourishes here in the near-virgin rainforest. Eleven species of native birds can be found here, and there is also a fascinating system of ancient caves that you can explore.

Mangaia: Said to be 18 million years old, the island of Mangaia is the most southerly in the Southern archipelago. Good for walks ashore, it is also a fascinating place to visit if you have any interest in archaeology or anthropology.

Level of skill

This area is not a cruising ground for the inexperienced. While its idyllic palm-fringed beaches, abundance of wildlife and laid-back lifestyle draw people in, the sailing can be very challenging and should only be attempted with proper care, attention and planning.

The remoteness of the Cook Islands is perhaps one of their biggest attractions, but it can also be a major hazard if the weather turns foul. There are only a few places of refuge here, with minimal space for visiting yachts. Studying the weather forecasts is essential, particularly if you plan to sail one of the longer passages between the islands, such as from Rarotonga to Palmerston, a distance of around 270nm, or you intend to anchor. While some of the anchorages offer good shelter, most are exposed from one direction or another. The moorings at Palmerston can also prove untenable if there is any north or west in the wind direction, and even the relative shelter of Rarotonga's main harbour at Avatiu can be unpleasant if there is any swell.

No yachts are allowed to stay within the harbour during the cyclone season, which runs from 1 November to 30 April, and occasionally you will be asked to leave if conditions look like they are going to deteriorate significantly during the main sailing season.

Another hazard to avoid is the coral, which grows in abundance within this area. Much of the archipelago is formed of coral atolls, and many of the islands are fringed with it, so careful pilotage is therefore essential to avoid running aground on it. Care should also be taken when dropping your anchor, as many anchors now litter the seabed having had to be cut free after getting jammed. Generally, however, the anchoring is good on sand, and the berthing is bow- or stern-to.

If the hazards haven't put you off, then this really is a wonderful place to explore if the conditions are right. The wildlife is incredible, the landscape stunning, and here you'll meet some of the genuinely nicest, most welcoming people in the world. The rewards are amazing, even if it is a trial to get there.

When to go

The Cook Islands enjoy a tropical climate, with a hot, dry season between May and November and a wet, humid season between December and April. Temperature variations are small between the two, with an average of 29°C (84°F) during the wet season and 25°C (77°F) during the dry season.

The islands lie within the South Pacific Convergence Zone, in an area that is susceptible to cyclones, and between November and March winds have been known to reach as high as 200km/h (124mph). Visiting boats are only welcome to cruise this area outside of the cyclone season, between May and October. Even yachts passing through on transit are discouraged from stopping here during the cyclone season. From May to October winds tend to be from the southeast, but sudden squalls often appear from any direction.

The remoteness of the islands means that relatively few people visit this area, so those that do are guaranteed a very warm welcome by the islanders, and a unique opportunity to explore the unexplored.

THE COOK ISLANDS AT A GLANCE

Route length: Around 900 miles.

Time required: Three to four weeks. Be aware that cruising permits only last 31 days, although they can be extended.

When to go: May to October.

Weather: Tropical climate. Wet, humid summers, with average temperatures of 29°C (84°F); dry winters with average temperatures of 25°C (77°F).

Type and size of boat: Power or sail, 30ft (9.1m) plus. Deep-draught boats that draw over 1.8m may struggle to enter some of the more shallow lagoons.

Equipment: Charts, chartplotter, depth sounder, binoculars, access to current weather forecasts, anchor, reliable engine.

Tides: The average tidal range is 0.6m, although it can rise to 1.1m at certain times of the year.

Hazards: Coral, reefs, swell, bad weather.

Suitable for night sailing: No.

Difficulty of route: Hard.

Skills required: Excellent meteorological, navigation and pilotage skills, and the ability to anchor in tricky conditions.

Charts: Admiralty: 4630 (Samoa Islands to Southern Cook Islands), 4657 (Southern Cook Islands to Îles de la Société and Îles Australes).

Berthing/mooring: Some bow- and stern-to berths at Aruntanga on Aitutaki and Avatiu on Rarotonga, although the latter can be susceptible to swell; mooring buoys at Palmerston; numerous anchorages elsewhere.

Ports of entry: Avatiu Harbour on Rarotonga, Arutanga on Aitutaki, Taunganui on Atiu.

Water: Available in Avatiu Harbour, Rarotonga.

Provisioning: Avatiu Harbour is the main source of provisioning within the Cook Islands. Limited chandlery, although some essential items can be imported to Avatiu from New Zealand. Fresh fruit and vegetables are available on Aitutaki.

Fuel: Available from Avatiu Harbour on Rarotonga. Fuel supplied by arrangement.

Shorepower: Avatiu Harbour, Rarotonga.

Maintenance: Crane and some facilities at Avatiu Harbour on Rarotonga.

Family friendliness: Very friendly and welcoming although good preparation is needed to ensure you have enough provisions. as well as the ability to entertain children/crew members during long passages.

Further reading: *Landfalls of Paradise: Cruising Guide to the Pacific Islands* by Earl R Hinz and Jim Howard; *Pacific Crossing Guide* by Michael Pocock and Ros Hogbin; *South Pacific Anchorages* by Warwick Clay.

Resources

right Cruising doesn't have to be expensive. Mljet is just one island in Croatia that provides numerous anchorages.

Formalities

Every country has its own formalities for entering and leaving, and paperwork that has to be completed or carried at all times. Before setting off on a particular cruise it is essential to research these clearance formalities in more detail.

This will not only save time when clearing in, but it will also prevent potential problems if you don't have the relevant paperwork. Some countries, such as Australia, even require you to notify them of your arrival in advance.

Documents that are most commonly required during clearance procedures include:
- Passports for skipper and all crew members, and visas where required, European Health Insurance Card (EHIC) if cruising in Europe
- Ship's papers, including registration document, insurance, proof of the vessel's VAT status, logbook detailing voyage, Ship Radio Licence
- Maritime Radio Operator's Certificate of Competence
- Cruising permits
- Documentation/certificates for diving gear

Be aware that failure to produce the relevant documentation when required can lead to hefty fines.

Some inland waterways, such as the French Canals (see p38–43), require the skipper to have an ICC (International Certificate of Competence). If you have a pet on board, then you must research regulations for bringing it into the country you intend to visit, including quarantine controls.

And finally, don't forget that on entering foreign waters you must fly the Q flag from your starboard shroud, as well as the country's courtesy ensign. Further details of ports of entry are included in the 'At a glance' sections.

Navigation

Before setting off, make sure you have the latest charts for the area that you intend to cruise. Imray and the Admiralty produce a wide choice of charts for European destinations, and some farther afield, but it is also worth finding out if there are any local charts as these may be more up to date or contain more detail.

Something else to consider when navigating is which IALA system is used in the country that you are sailing in. The IALA system is an internationally recognized scheme that enables sailors to identify and understand navigational buoys and marks, regardless of where they are in the world. However, to confuse matters, the IALA system is divided into two regions – IALA A, which is used throughout Europe and much of the rest of the world, and IALA B, which is used in the USA and the Pacific Rim – and while some of the marks, such as cardinal marks, have identical meanings in both regions, lateral channel marks don't. Check which region you are in before setting of as, for example, a red buoy seen in European waters can mean something completely different in the USA.

below Having a well-found boat is essential, especially if cruising in rock-strewn areas such as the Lofoten Islands.

Safety

It shouldn't need to be said, but all the cruises in this book require a well-found boat in good condition and with a comprehensive inventory of equipment on board. Specific equipment required for particular cruises is included within the 'At a glance' sections, but in general you should ensure that the following safety gear is carried on board:

Lifejackets and safety harness/line for each crew member • Heaving line • Torch • Dan buoy • Personal Locator Beacons • VHF Radio • Flares • Lifebuoy • Radar reflector • Bucket • Foghorn • First-aid kit • For longer passages, such as the Atlantic crossing, a liferaft and EPIRB are also essential.

When to go

Some destinations have year-round sailing seasons, others have long sailing seasons, and others have short seasons, so plan your cruise carefully. It is also important to consider your arrival and departure times at a destination if it forms part of a longer cruise, as some areas – such as the Atlantic and Bay of Biscay – should be avoided at all costs when gales or hurricanes are

common. Many of the routes can be tricky if the weather turns nasty, owing to the proximity of rocks, lee shores and strong tidal currents, so make sure you consult the forecast before planning your cruise. If you are looking for a bit of seclusion, then find out when peak season is, to avoid arriving at the same time as the crowds.

Budgets

How much a cruise will cost is a question that is almost impossible to answer, as it will vary from boat to boat, crew to crew, and destination to destination. The only possible answer is 'as much or as little as you want'. Cruising doesn't have to be expensive, and experience has shown you can get by on a modest budget. If you are happy to anchor off and dinghy ashore, or choose town quays with free berthing, then you won't have to spend much at all, but if you want to plug in to shorepower every night, have hot and cold showers on tap and walk-ashore access to the finest restaurants and bars, then start saving. The routes in this book offer a variety of options. Most include at least one marina, but they are rarely the only choice as there are normally plenty of anchorages. Plan your route carefully, and you'll be surprised how far your budget will go.

Further reading

Europe

The Adlard Coles Book of Mediterranean Cruising by Rod Heikell

Adriatic Pilot by T & D Thompson

Atlantic Spain & Portugal by RCCPF, Martin Walker & Henry Buchanan

The Baltic Sea by RCC Pilotage Foundation

The Croatia Cruising Companion by Jane Cody & John Nash

Cruise the Black Sea by Doreen & Archie Annan

Cruising French Waterways by Hugh McKnight

Cruising Galicia by Carlos Rojas & Robert Bailey

Cruising the Inland Waterways of France & Belgium by M Harwood, B Davison & R Edgar

Cruising Scotland by Mike Balmforth & Edward Mason

Floating Through France by Brenda Davison

The Fluvial guides to the French Waterways

Inland Waterways of France by David Edwards-May

Ionian by Rod Heikell

Ionian Cruising Companion by Vanessa Bird

Isles of Scilly Pilot by Graham Adam

Italian Waters Pilot by Rod Heikell

Magic Turkey by Alfredo Giacon

Mediterranean France and Corsica Pilot by Rod & Lucinda Heikell

Norway by Judy Lomax/RCC Pilotage Foundation

Norwegian Cruising Guide by John Armitage & Mark Brackenbury

Norwegian Cruising Guide by Phyllis L Nickel & John H Harries

NP255 Tidal Stream Atlas – Falmouth to Padstow (including the Isles of Scilly)

Outer Hebrides by Clyde Cruising Club

River Seine Cruising Guide by Derek Bowskill

777 Harbours & Anchorages by Karl H Bestanding

South Biscay Pilot by RCCPF/Steve Pickard

Through the French Canals by David Jefferson

Turkey Cruising Companion by Emma Watson

Turkish Waters & Cyprus Pilot by Rod & Lucinda Heikell

Waterstops Through France by Bill & Laurel Cooper

West Country Cruising Companion by Mark Fishwick

The Western Isles by Martin Lawrence

Western North Atlantic & Caribbean

Atlantic Crossing Guide by RCC Pilotage Foundation

Atlantic Sailors' Handbook by Alastair Buchan

Charlie's Charts Western Mexico by Charles E Wood

A Cruising Guide to Puget Sound and the San Juan Islands: Olympia to Port Angeles by Migael Scherer

A Cruising Guide to the Virgin Islands by Stephen J Pavlidis
Cruising Guides to the Virgin Islands by Simon & Nancy Scott
Dreamspeaker Volume 4 – The San Juan Islands by Anne & Laurence Yeadon-Jones
Grenada to the Virgin Islands by Jacques Patuelli
The Intracoastal Waterway by Jan & Bill Moeller
The Intracoastal Waterway Chartbook by International Marine
The Mexico Boating Guide by Patricia Rains
Sailing an Atlantic Circuit by Alastair Buchan
Sailor's Guide to the Windward Islands by Chris Doyle
Sea of Cortez, a Cruiser's Guidebook by Shawn Breeding
Street's Guide Puerto Rico, Passage & Virgin Islands by Don Street
Virgin Islands NV-Cruising Guide by NV Charts
Windward Anchorages by Chris Doyle
World Cruising Routes by Jimmy Cornell
Your First Atlantic Crossing by Les Weatheritt

South Pacific

Coastal Cruising Handbook by Royal Arakana Yacht Club
Cruising the Coral Coast by Alan Lucas
Destination NZ – Blue Water Cruisers Guide New Zealand's Northern Waters by Graham Brice & Christopher Carey
Landfalls of Paradise: Cruising Guide to the Pacific Islands by Earl R Hinz & Jim Howard
100 Magic Miles of Great Barrier Reef: The Whitsunday Islands by David Colfelt
Pacific Crossing Guide by Michael Pocock & Ros Hogbin
South Pacific Anchorages by Warwick Clay
Whitsundays Book by David Colfelt

South-East Asia & Indian Ocean

Indian Ocean Cruising Guide by Rod Heikell
Seychelles Nautical Pilot by Alain Rondeau
South-East Asia Pilot (Imray)

General reading

Going Foreign by Barry Pickthall
The Illustrated Boat Dictionary in 9 Languages by Vanessa Bird
Sailing in Paradise by Rod Heikell
World Cruising Destinations by Jimmy Cornell
World Cruising Routes by Jimmy Cornell

Websites

www.noonsite.com
www.cruising.org.uk

Index

Acknowledgements

The publisher would like to thank the following for their kind permission to reproduce photographs in this book (Abbreviations key: t = top, b = bottom, r = right, l = left)

Alamy: 7, 12, 23, 24, 52, 70, 73, 88, 98, 101, 102, 103, 107, 112, 113, 119, 140, 149, 150

Corbis: 59, 72

Getty Images: 11, 29, 30, 53, 55, 90, 100, 120, 146, 150

Robyn Chamberlain-Webber: 142

Russell Sturmey: 118

Shutterstock: 4, 6, 8, 10, 13, 14, 16, 17, 18, 19, 20, 22, 25, 26, 28, 31, 32, 34, 35, 36, 37, 38, 40, 41, 42, 43, 44, 46, 47, 48, 49, 50, 54, 56, 58, 59, 60, 61, 62, 64, 65, 66, 67, 68, 71, 74, 76, 77, 78, 79, 80, 82, 83, 84, 85, 86, 89, 91, 92, 94, 95, 96, 97, 104, 106, 108, 109, 110, 114, 115, 116, 121, 122, 124, 125, 126, 127, 128, 130, 131, 132, 133, 134, 136, 137, 138, 139, 143, 144, 145, 148, 152, 153, 154, 155, back cover

Front cover image: Getty Images

Locations of background and header images:
P11: Isle of Barra
P13: Stornoway Harbour
P18: Moskensøya, Lofoten
P19: Fishing harbour of Sørland
P23: Grinda Island
P25: Vaxholm fortress
P29: Rocky beach
P31: Little islands near Helsinki
P35: Granite rocks, Hankö
P37: Falmouth
P41: Vineyard near River Marne
P43: Sète harbour
P47: Bay of Villefranche
P49: Port of Marseille
P53: Frouxeira, near La Coruña
P55: Camariñas, Galicia
P59: Aeolian Islands
P61: Syracuse
P65: Murter Island beach
P67: Kostrina cove
P71: Ionian sea
P73: Pantokratoras Castle, Preveza town
P77: Kalkan, Antalya
P79: Marmaris city
P83: Sunset near St Lucia
P85: Las Palmas, Gran Canaria
P89: Tobago Cays beach
P91: Tobago Cays
P95: Tortola
P97: Norman Island
P101: Bahía Concepcíon, Sea of Cortez
P103: Puerto Escondido
P107: Lummi Island, Bellingham Bay
P109: Lopez Island
P113: Key West, Florida
P115: Albemarle Sound
P119: Manitoulin Island
P121: Manitoulin Island
P125: Krabi
P127: Koh Lanta Island
P131: Grand Anse beach
P133: Source d'Argent
P137: Rangitoto Island
P139: Russell Wharf
P143: Whitsunday Islands
P145: Hamilton Island
P149: Palmerston Atoll
P150: Palmerston Atoll